Chamomile and Lavender
Sips of Peace, Comfort, and Introspection

Chamomile

Noun
: A herb celebrated for its calming effects and healing properties, symbolizing tranquility and the gentle encouragement to let go of tension, inviting peace into one's life.

Lavender

Noun
: A fragrant herb valued for its soothing scent and restorative benefits, representing purification, comfort, and the soothing of spirit and body.

Peace

Noun
: A condition of tranquility and serenity that transcends external circumstances, offering a deep sense of harmony within oneself and with the world.

Comfort

Noun
: The state of physical ease and freedom from pain or constraint; the alleviation of a person's feelings of grief or distress, providing solace and a sense of safety.

Introspection

Noun
: The examination or observation of one's own mental and emotional processes, fostering a deeper understanding of oneself and facilitating personal growth and self-awareness.

Contents

Prelude

What is it about sipping hot tea,
That calms the world, letting the mind roam free?

Dear warriors, seekers, friends, lovers, sisters, and brothers,

Welcome to an interactive journey of the senses, where the pages of *"Chamomile & Lavender: Sips of Peace, Comfort, and Introspection"* unfold like a gentle embrace, offering solace and understanding in the quiet moments of your day.

My journey to creating this velvety book began as I wandered through the shadows of *grief's quiet garden*, finding profound comfort in the simple, yet transformative, act of sipping Chamomile and Lavender tea. This ritual became my sanctuary, allowing me to breathe, reflect, and gradually **see the colors of the rainbow again—it is the essence of tea, the tea without the tea**, if you will, embodying moments of deep reflection and inviting you into a world of contemplation and calm.

While the book emerges from navigating the complexities of grief, it **celebrates the full spectrum of human experience**—from the joys and loves that uplift us to the sorrows and vulnerabilities that connect us. Designed to mirror those moments of introspection, it offers comfort and companionship through shared experiences.

This labor of love is a testament to the beauty and resilience found in embracing every facet of our being, reminding us of the vibrant hues that follow life's storms. Ultimately, I believe that peace and comfort don't just come to you through cozy words but often through profound experiences and feeling seen and heard through shared stories and moments.

As you wander through these pages, I invite you to view this book not just as a collection of poetry and prose but as a **companion on your own journey toward healing, understanding, and self-discovery.** It's a dialogue between us, bridging our experiences through the universal language of emotion, and like a supportive friend, **I am here with you, offering love & hugs and rooting for you every step of the way!**

Continued

This book is infused with elements intended to accompany you through the complexities that introspection can evoke.

Here's a brief guide to navigating these waters:

- **Affirmations** centered on the page and italicized, are grounding mantras here to accompany you through reflection, offer comfort, and inspire your daily journey. They are designed to help you embody empowerment and confidently work through what comes up for you.

- **Touchpoints of Calm** marked by chamomile tea tabs, are invitations for you to pause, reflect, or simply be. Amidst the ebb and flow of emotions, these points serve as your quiet harbors.

- **Bitter Truths** challenge you to face life's realities with courage and openness. They offer unvarnished insights into life's complexities. Interspersed throughout, these truths are meant to resonate when you need them most, serving as mirrors for self-reflection. I have chosen not to label them explicitly; they will find you, guiding you toward deeper understanding and resilience.

- **Pen, Ponder, or Pass (PPP)** at each chapter's end offers reflective questions to deepen your self-exploration. Since there isn't technically enough room to write in the book, I encourage you to use a dedicated journal for this journey. Journal, reflect, revisit later, or simply pass—the choice is yours. This book honors your unique journey and the way you choose to navigate it.

- **Checklists** provide thematic insights and practical advice to enrich your journey, offering support without dictating your path. Draw inspiration or simply contemplate their suggestions.

Continued

Although this book is crafted with structure, I encourage you to **let your intuition guide your journey** through these pages as you immerse yourself in the poetry, prose, and interactive elements. There's no set path—<u>**dive in wherever your heart feels the pull.**</u> Each element is designed for you to engage with on your terms, offering moments of peace, comfort, and introspection.

In addition, you will find:

- <u>**Resources for Healing and Hope:**</u> Starting **on page 415**, there is a curated list of mental health resources provided at the book's end to support those seeking further guidance.

  Remember, reaching out for help is a courageous step toward healing and growth.

- <u>**Tea Recipes:**</u> The book concludes with specially crafted tea recipes, starting **on page 421**, each reflecting the essence of the chapters you've explored. Inspired by the solace found in the ritual of tea-making, these recipes invite you to add a sensory layer to your reflective journey, encouraging you to create meaningful blends of your own.

This book mirrors my journey from darkness into light, and I hope it serves as a beacon on your path as well—a testament to the strength, hope, and beauty found in embracing every facet of your being. Together, let us celebrate the vivid colors of life, where each emotion is acknowledged, savored, and respected just like each sip of your favorite brew.

In the spirit of shared introspection and growth, I welcome you. Let's embark on this journey together, with the warmth of chamomile and lavender guiding our way.

With warmth and gratitude,

Sonesta Wilde

Chapters

In Quiet Moments of Introspection...

Touchpoint of Calm Index

Navigate to your moments of calm with ease. Below you will find a list of all the touchpoints of calm provided throughout this book, along with their page numbers. **Each entry is marked with a chamomile tab**, designed like a "save for later" icon adorned with a chamomile flower, symbolizing solace, safety, and calm.

Use this index and the tabs to quickly find guidance, reflection, or a quiet moment whenever you need it.

Before you begin, please note:
While this book offers moments of peace and introspection, it also
explores the depths of grief, trauma, and mental health challenges,
with references to suicide and abuse. These topics are handled with
care but may be triggering for some readers. If you are sensitive to
these themes, please take care of yourself and proceed with caution.
For additional resources or support, refer to page 416 or reach out to
a mental health professional.

Always remember, it's okay to not be okay.
It's okay to ask for help. It's more than okay—
it's a courageous step forward.

Pour Me Sunshine

A New Day Brewed with Hope and Endless Possibilities

Why hold onto the garments of yesterday
When today offers a wardrobe of new possibilities?

With the retreat of the dark sky,
dawn's gentle graze sends chills
crawling down my back,
mirroring the cold indifference of the night.

Yet a truth lingers in the fog:
dwelling on yesterday's frost only deprives you
of the comforting warmth today brings.

Invite happiness in;
don't let it remain
a stranger lingering
at your door.

Seasons of Release

The moment at the onset of fall is when seasons seem to clash — it is as though it is grasping at the lingering warmth of summer while simultaneously being drawn by the crisp breeze rustling the descending leaves.

Yet, in its own time, nature gracefully yields. It releases what was and embraces what is to come: a season of change, a time for letting go of what must be released.

Sometimes
you need to go,
even when there
is nowhere to go.
Because where you are,
is not where you should be.

Trust your inner compass,
let intuition light your way;
It whispers of places where
your heart is meant to stay.

If only I could be like the sun,
casting its light on all it sees.
With its energy and hope,
I wish to seize.

It knows that while it might
cast shadows that weep,
its strength is in its glow,
harnessing the promise
that a new day brings.

// glowing ambitions

Darling,

I hope you believe
in the pure goodness of your soul,
in the way your smile rivals the radiance
of the stars.

How your embrace can soothe the deepest scars
of those who have yearned for genuine love and care.

I hope you see the universe within yourself,
a galaxy of wonders, of kindness, of strength.

May you always know your irreplaceable worth,
and believe, with every sunrise,
in the magic you bring to this world.

You are not just a part of the cosmos;
you are a cosmos in yourself,
and I hope you believe that,
deeply and truly.

I am a radiant being, filled with kindness, strength, and irreplaceable worth.

I see the universe within myself and embrace my unique magic.

With every sunrise, I believe in the goodness of my soul and the love and light I bring to the world.

You deserve this:

You deserve to find healing from the burdens that keep you up at night, to discover solace in the quiet moments when the world is still, and to embrace a sense of inner peace that gently carries you through twilight's deepest sigh.

Love,
you are the world.
No need to carry it too.
Put it down and rest,
so you can
rise.

People may doubt your capabilities,
proclaiming with certainty that you won't succeed.

Yet, their assertions only hold truth
if you let their skepticism seep into your belief.

Become rooted,
like the mighty oak—
resilient,
always returning
with a fresh face,
unshaken
by the frost of winter,
nor swayed by leaves shed
in yesterday's storm.

Embrace what you need today:

Today, I choose to embody _____

Resilience
Love
Silliness
Strength
Capability
Peace
Inspiration
Playfulness
Assertiveness
Bravery
Wellness
Joy
Groundedness
Hope
Creativity
Empowerment
Nurturance
Value
Freedom

There is something
enchanting hovering
in the mist
of the morning hours,
a sworn testament
whispered by the rustling leaves,
echoed by the melodies
of the birds' first songs.

I Hope to
See You at Sunrise

You still have so much to live for,
so please, be generous with yourself.

Forgive yourself. Practice patience.
Hold space for your own needs and feelings.

Yes, life can be overwhelmingly hard,
and I know it feels like your world is ablaze.
But remember, **without** your light,
the world would be a much colder place.

Fan those flames with courage.
Put on your finest shades —
to face the vibrancy of your future
and walk the path that is paved.

As you journey forward...

Today,
Tomorrow,
And every day that follows,
I hope to see you there —
being embraced by each rising sun.

And in its warmth,
may you find the strength to keep going,
the hope to see through the smoke,
and the promise of brighter days ahead.

For the anxious mind:

No amount of worry or rumination is going to shield you from reality.

You can't live in the present if you're dwelling on experiences that haven't happened yet.

You are more than you give yourself credit for. Trust that, should the time come when you are faced with a challenge, you will find a way through.

Remember, you have survived every single day up to this moment.
It hasn't always been easy, has it?
But you've always, always made it through.

Give a voice to your deepest wounds.
Let them sing of your darkest tunes.

Let them be the song that heals your soul,
Where broken pieces become whole.

In the symphony of sorrow, find your grace,
For in every note, there's a sacred place.

Here the heart begins to mend
and the radiant sun nourishes you within.

I embrace each new day and the radiant light that nourishes my soul.

I honor my journey, knowing that through expression I find healing and strength.

If your sorrow could speak, what would it say?

When the world asks more than you can give, know that:

It's okay if the only feeling alive within you
is the drum, fervently beating from your chest.

It's okay if your only capacity today
is to lie down, embracing a moment of rest.

*Simply waking up and facing a new day
is an achievement in itself.*

Every morning,
I greet the sunrise
through my broken blinds,
yet in a mere blink,
the evening has already intertwined.

Time's flow remains a mystery,
its fleeting nature, a constant history.

I don't understand where the time goes.
I don't understand where the time goes.

The In-Between

The contrast of light and dark is unclear:
I feel like a deer, caught
in the headlights of my own life,
frozen, in moments of doubt,
where shadows and beams collide.
Each heartbeat echoes uncertainty
as I grapple with which highway to ride,
yearning for clarity, for a sign,
to get me through the day.
I'm lost between sun's warmth
and night's cool sway.
Yet, deep within, a whisper calls,
urging me to find my way,
to navigate this in-between—
the dance of dawn
and dusky gray.

If you no longer feel at home,
make sure that your home wasn't solely built within
someone else.

In the quiet corners of your heart, you might feel a certain emptiness. It's as if you've poured parts of yourself into **building someone else's world** – laying bricks, crafting walls, even shaping windows to peer out at a life that wasn't quite your own.

Now, standing in the midst of what feels like an emotional void, take a moment. Reflect on the energy, the love, the essence you invested elsewhere. It's time to redirect that back to yourself. Like gathering fallen leaves, **collect the pieces of your spirit you've scattered.** Each fragment holds a power, a piece of your story, your being.

Begin the gentle task of rebuilding, not with stone or mortar, but with the **resilience and warmth** that live within you. Construct not just a shelter, but a place of solace and strength in your own soul. Let each memory, each learned lesson become a stepping stone to a renewed sense of self.

In this journey of reclamation, **you are both the architect and the sanctuary.** In the quiet rebuilding, find a home within yourself – a place where every corridor leads back to a heart full of self-love and peace.

Not every sunrise will be basked in joy;
sometimes, they demand resilience.

Each day I wake,
I make up my bed.
I see fragments lying there
of dreams that are dead.

And in the quiet of dawn,
those fragments speak clear,
announcing whispers of hopes,
and what I hold dear—

to take my dreams with me
before I smother them with my sheets,
even if they've been through the storm.

For in their resilience, in their renew,
lies the promise of a brighter morn.

Get up.
Get out.
And go for a walk.

How might you carry the fragments of your dreams into your day, even those that feel tattered or worn by past struggles?

Where there is dark,
Let there be light.

And that prism of hope
Will bring you life.

Ordinary Magic

Morning news
Golden hues
The smell of French toast
Listening to classic tunes

Crisp mornings
Fuzzy socks
Gentle nudges
Passionate talks

Kid cartoons
Lunch with friends at noon
These nourishing moments
Craft our finest tunes

Greet the day with open arms.
Let the sunrays shine in.

Touchpoint of Calm:
Sunrise Flight

Visualize:
Birds taking flight against the backdrop of a radiant sunrise. Each wingbeat lifts away the remnants of night, ushering in the purity and potential of a new day.

Feel:
The gentle warmth of the rising sun on your skin, dissolving any lingering shadows of doubt or worry.

Embrace:
Open your heart to the day's possibilities. With each breath, draw in the fresh morning air, filling your soul with renewed energy and optimism.

BE
like wildflowers
dancing to *their favorite tunes*
embracing
the everchanging melody
of
the
w
i
n
d

Plant Gardens,
Not Wastelands

We often hear about being the villain in someone else's story.

Yet, it's equally crucial that you're not assigning yourself that role in your own narrative.

Speak to your heart with **words that cultivate flowers**, not thorns, that mend tattered roots, not fray them.

Be your own sunshine, too.

Light up the darker corners of your self-perception with warmth and kindness—fostering **deeply rooted love** and growth from within.

I hope that even in the rainy seasons
The sun will shine through.

I know it will
I just hope you see it too.

To be honest,
Swimming was never my forte.
But I have embraced this sea of sorrow,
Making friends with the waves.

Drowning is not the way.

Just as Mother Earth
moves through her seasons,
you too hold the power to flourish–
to bloom with the vibrancy of spring
and to radiate with the brilliance of summer.

And when your winters arrive,
as they inevitably will,
remember that it's okay to turn inward,
and to embrace a period of hibernation.

For even the most splendid blooms
were once mere seedlings,
patiently gathering their strength in the quiet,
supportive embrace of the dark,
preparing to emerge into the light
when the time is right.

I woke up,
nearly tumbling out of my bed.
The room was as dark as **crow eyes**
from my blackout blinds.
I tried to raise them,
but the cord snapped instead.
Tossing the frayed string onto my wine-stained bohemian rug,
I sighed with dismay.
"Here we go again."
Yet, as I looked over, a beam of light was shining,
piercing the gloom on the floor.
It reminded me: that though my soul may feel tattered and torn,
without the dark,
the light wouldn't shine as before,
and with each new dawn,
there's a chance to be reborn.

Unfolding Horizons:
Tales of Steady Growth

'Slow and steady wins the race,' they often say,
a notion ripe with both truth and cliché.

Each morning brings its own subtle change,
some days brighter, some a little strange.

Yet, as time gently unfolds its steady hand,
a silent metamorphosis quietly takes its stand.

A glance in the mirror
on a seemingly ordinary day,
reveals a broader smile,
a heart lighter in every way.

Your once pain-filled heart
now sings a different tune,
of strength, hope, and gratitude,
a soul in bloom.

It's a reminder that life's path,
though sometimes grey,
leads to brighter horizons,
in its own unassuming way.

Chamomile and Lavender:
Sips of Healing and Hope

I still remember the moment
my heart opened up.
I grabbed the box of chamomile
and lavender tea,
sat down, and poured a cup.

I took a moment to reflect on the pain
that had devoured me over the past few months,
the sadness that consumed me,
the moments I needed a hug.

As I inhaled the tranquil aroma,
with my hands wrapped in warmth,
it was as though with each sniff
and sip that followed,
my heart, which felt it would never heal,
started to open up.

And by the time my cup
was ever so cool to the touch,
I realized that in between that moment—
when the night sky kisses away the day—
there is hope upon the horizon,
and the sun will rise again.

Words that renew your spirit:

Revival
Rebirth
Awakening
Clarity
Enlightenment
Inspiration
Vitality
Refreshment
Restoration
Renewal

You Can Hurt, Heal,
and Thrive at the Same Time

In our journey of self-discovery, healing and thriving exist not as opposites but as harmonious companions. This journey mirrors the nuances of nature itself.

Consider a tree's resilience: enduring through seasons, losing branches yet growing stronger. Or reflect on a fallen flower, which, in its withering, enriches the soil for new life.

Nature's adaptability, its embrace of change, serves as a profound reminder for us.

In the ebb and flow of our own lives, we too encounter moments of loss, times when it seems we are shedding parts of our essence.

Yet, in these phases of unbecoming, our most significant growth often occurs.

We heal, we flourish, and through this, we engage in a continuous process of **becoming and unbecoming**, all intertwined. This cycle transcends mere recovery or progress; it represents transformation and rediscovery. It's about embracing every aspect of our existence with acceptance and grace, recognizing that pain, healing, and growth can coexist, each shaping our journey in its unique way.

This morning, I choose to embrace the sunrise,
becoming the Picasso of my unfolding day.
I paint portraits of hope on the blank horizon,
feeling energized with each vibrant brushstroke
as I complement the sun's golden play.

Tears of joy fall from my eyes like confetti when I:

- Sit and celebrate the woman I have become
- Cherish the peace I've made with a past that can't be undone
- Revel in the excitement for all that is yet to come

Remember:
Even the darkest nights break with the promise of dawn.

Checklist:
<u>Crafting the First Notes of the Day</u>

○   **Greet the Morning Light:** Welcome the day with a heart of gratitude. In the quiet hush of early light, find a single thing in the morning's touch to be grateful for, a small joy to hold close.

○   **Define Your Sunrise Purpose:** With the dawn's first gleam, carve out an intention. Let this early light ignite a goal or aspiration, guiding your steps through the day's unfolding path.

○   **Renew with the New Dawn:** Add a fresh, positive element to your morning routine, symbolizing the rebirth offered by each new day. Embrace this change as a reflection of dawn's refreshing energy and the endless possibilities it brings.

○   **Morning Reflection:** Take a few moments in the early morning to reflect on a recent lesson or insight. How can this newfound wisdom shape your approach to the day ahead?

– Pen, Ponder, or Pass –
Dawn's Fresh Beginnings

Reflect on Gratitude: What was one moment from this morning that you felt truly grateful for, however small it might have been? How did acknowledging this moment make you feel?

Visualize Your Intentions: Imagine setting a positive intention for today. What might that intention be, and how could it influence your day? This is a moment to think about the kind of day you wish to create.

Exploring New Beginnings: If you were to add a new element to your morning routine that could enhance your day, what would it be? Why do you think this change could be beneficial?

Morning Light: How does the morning light influence your mood and energy? Reflect on the way sunlight, or the lack thereof, affects the start of your day and your overall outlook.

Pour Me
Strength in the Rain

Steeping Strength and Courage Amidst Stormy Skies

In solidarity with your journey:

In the quiet moments when the rain whispers outside, know that your heartbeats are heard. Each challenge, each tear, is a testament to your journey, a journey marked by resilience and courage.

You carry within you an inner strength, a quiet yet powerful force that can weather any storm. Remember, it's okay to seek shelter, to find comfort in the arms of others or the pages of a story.

Your bravery in facing life's tempests is admirable. Hold onto hope, for after the rain comes the promise of clearer skies.

What hurts?
What has the power to heal?

- *You*

Everyone seems okay
until they don't.
Because we rarely see that other side,
hidden behind veils of 'just fine.'

If only we would
let each other in a little deeper,
a little more often,
just for a little while,
we would see
that we are all bleeding
from little cuts,
and wounds we don't quite know how to heal.

Yet, in plain sight, we've each found
our own way to cover these scars,
by finding the right shade of a bandage,
and masking our pain with a semblance of normalcy.

If only we dared to reveal our true selves,
we might find solace in our shared struggles,
and **healing in the honesty** of our collective vulnerabilities.

A tear-saturated sky
harbors the promise of peace and renewal.

Within each gust of sorrow,
find resilience in moments of stillness.

Together, in our shared sorrows,
we quench the earth's thirst,
fostering a quiet resilient strength
that blossoms into a garden of hope,
flourishing in the wake of the storm.

Touchpoint of Calm:
Rhythms of the Rain

Visualize:

Imagine standing firm under an umbrella amidst the rain, symbolizing your own resilience and protection. Watch as the rain falls rhythmically around you, each drop contributing to nature's soothing lullaby.

Listen and Breathe:

Close your eyes and tune into the sound of rain tapping gently on surfaces. As you listen, inhale for four counts, hold for four counts, and exhale for four counts. Match your breathing to the steady, soothing rhythm of the rain, allowing it to ground you in the present moment.

Each raindrop,
a whispered secret,
from the clouds above—
"Hey, remember when you shrugged off
Mom's loving nudge to check the weather?"

Ah,
the clouds,
playful pranksters of the sky,
chuckling at our oversight,
as they spill their gathered tears.

The vast expanse of time may seem as though it stretches endlessly before us, yet its bounds are unknown, its end unpredictably fixed. A truth we may only come to understand when it's too late.

He said, 'I have time,'
with the certainty of one who believes
it's a resource he owns.
Yet, time is the elusive current
we all swim in,
not a commodity we can clutch.
It flows through our fingers,
through our lives,
with indifferent persistence.

The notion of 'having time'
is a **soothing illusion that often
lulls us into complacency.**

Time has us, relentlessly moving forward,
and our true power lies not in possession
but in choice.

How we spend these fleeting moments,
the present we are so graciously allotted—
that's where our true influence lies.

Even amid the chaotic storm,
hope quietly blossoms on the other side.

If a storm could reveal an inner truth,
what would you wish to discover?

Suddenly, without a whisper of warning,
my world ignites into a ruthless wildfire.
Voraciously consuming everything
I thought I knew,
leaving behind only haze
and ashes of a once clear,
vibrant existence.

Now cold,
I drift like a ghost through the remnants.
Yet, in time, I find myself reborn.
From new earth and sown seeds,
fertilized by the tears that once
cleansed my sorrow,
I begin to sprout anew.

Despite the engulfing chaos,
I retain the essence of me.
And that — that steadfast spirit — is all
I will ever truly need,
even as I navigate the tender journey
of relearning who 'me' is.

His words become quicksand in my mind,
ensnaring my thoughts with a relentless grip.

I'm stuck,
unable to break free,
and in no time
I feel myself
rapidly
losing
it all.

I've been drowning in the desert,

Climbing mountains on the plains,

Flying in the ocean,
And swimming in space.

We belong together, apart.

Nothing

      makes

   sense

any

   m

     o

      r

      e

#$^@#fe66&$*

The loss of trust in those we once leaned on can shake the very ground beneath us. The foundation, once deemed solid and safe for holding our heart, begins to crumble, leaving us scrambling for balance amidst the unexpected tremors of betrayal and change.

It's a jarring realization, as relationships that seemed unbreakable start to fissure, forcing us to navigate a new, uncertain landscape.

In this upheaval, we find ourselves grappling with the fragments of what we thought was steadfast, searching for solid ground in a world that has suddenly shifted under our feet.

With them you were good.

Without them <u>you are great.</u>

Can a heart, once broken,
Truly lose its form?

Or does each crack echo a love
That once was warm?

Within its breaks, a testament,
Of every ache it rose above.

Yes, a heart is still a heart,
Indomitable at its core.

There is power in your pain.

You can use that power to break you.
Or to move mountains and ascend to your highest self.

The choice is yours.

Touchpoint of Calm:
After the Rain

Visualize:
Imagine an umbrella standing firm amidst the rain, symbolizing your own protection and endurance. Envision the rain falling rhythmically around you, each drop a beat in nature's soothing lullaby.

Listen:
Close your eyes and focus on the sound of the rain. Notice the varied tempos and volumes as the rain taps gently on surfaces around you. Let these sounds ground you in the present, turning the rhythm into a meditative experience that reinforces your resilience amidst life's storms.

*I am free to be patient with myself
as I work through my past regrets and mistakes.*

Shedding the past:

Do not let anyone shroud you in the cloak of your past. The journey
you have traveled has transformed you; the person you once were has
evolved into a version that **no longer exists**. It's a common struggle –
others may find it hard to accept the magnitude of your growth.

Remember, it's *not your responsibility* to alter their perceptions.

Your progress, your change, is for you to embrace and for them to
witness when they choose to look beyond their veil of assumptions
and judgments. **If they fail to see the light of your evolution**, it's a
sign that their role in your story is limited.

Your path forward is one of self-recognition and acceptance,
unimpeded by the doubts of others.

The tips of my fingers,
Are glazed with the tears,
That taught me how to heal,
Let go, and release my fears.

In every drop of rain,
a fallen flower finds its strength.

Words that empower:

Courage
Determination
Strength
Resilience
Confidence
Perseverance
Boldness
Vigor
Tenacity
Fortitude

Oh,
how beautiful it is
learning how to fly
even with clipped wings.

Singing 'Hallelujah,
thank you, Jesus,'
and I'm not even religious.

Sit still
and listen
to the tender
symphony
of the rain,
a lullaby
for weary hearts
and unmet hopes.
Offering a gentle reminder
that from sadness,
new strength can cultivate
and sprout.

It's not the presence of stress
that defines our journey,
but the art of navigating through it.

Stress, in itself, isn't the enemy;
it's a signpost, a marker of the challenges
that prompt us to grow and evolve.

As we acknowledge each stressor,
we're invited to dance with our resilience,
to engage in the fluid movement
from tension to release,
from effort to ease.

It's in this dance that we find our strength,
that we learn the rhythms of self-care and self-compassion.

Touchpoint of Calm:
Moving Through Stress

Pause for a moment:
Close your eyes and take a deep breath. Envision yourself as a willow, swaying gracefully in the wind, bending but not breaking under the weight of the world. With each exhalation, release a thread of tension, and with each inhalation, draw in the calm of knowing you are resilient.

Visualize:
Imagine a calm lake at dawn, the surface so still it reflects the world like a mirror. You are that lake, your depths rich with the power to reflect, absorb, and transform each ripple of stress into a wave of peace.

Remember:
The goal isn't to eliminate stress but to learn the graceful art of moving with it, recognizing that after each ebb, there's a flow, after each release, a return to tranquility.

Step by step,
day by day,
I move forward,
embracing the journey.

I may tumble,
I may fall,
but I will rise,
by the end of it all.

Raindrops pitter-patter
against the windowpane—
gentle reminders from Mother Nature
that even she has moments of tears.

And if she can turn her sorrows
into life-giving waters, so can we.

Though, admittedly,
I'd prefer if her tears
would spare the hours
of my picnic under the sun.

The irony isn't lost upon the track—
How many yearn for the finish line,
Yet stand reluctant at the race's start—
Seeking the end without a journey,
Victory without the scars.

We run away from our problems with the roots of them
intertwining our shoelaces.

Running away from our problems
only tightens the knot at the core.
To face our problems is our true pace;
within every challenge, a lesson is stored.

Each stride we take
reminds us they are not finished with us yet.
But as we confront them,
they begin to untangle the mess,
unveiling newfound freedom and paths less traveled—
our journey to feeling our absolute best.

10,000 steps a day
I can only hope they are all in the right direction.

Ten thousand steps a day—so goes the prevailing wisdom
for sound health.

I really wonder who comes up with this stuff.

Nonetheless, as the pedometer ticks closer to the day's goal, I can't
help but muse: What's the real aim here? Is this path leading me in a
meaningful direction, or am I just pacing the same old loop?

Every step unfolds into a moment of reflection, a fleeting meditation
on the apparent path to wellness that I have carved out for myself.
Some steps are buoyed with assurance, while others seem to sink
under the weight of hesitation.

When the sun dips below the horizon and my step counter applauds
my accomplishments—sure, hitting the target is great and all. But the
more pressing ponderance is: Is this daily journey drawing me any
closer to my heart's truest desires, towards my soul's earnest purpose?

Are you a victim in the chaos
drawn by your own hand?

Before you pass on your problems,
ponder—might you hold the key?
In your grasp, perhaps,
the resolution is nestled—
within the power of your hands.

// own your story
// embrace accountability
// be the architect of your solutions

Let's not live without truly living.

The pain of failing is far less
than the pain of never trying at all.

Choose your hard.

Sometimes you win;
Sometimes you realize —
life isn't a competition.

The only battle you should conquer
is the fight for the love
you need to have for yourself.

Well, I've come to understand that while I may not know exactly where my footsteps will lead, standing still has never gotten me anywhere. So, I'll embrace the uncertainty, continue this journey in motion, and trust that as long as I move with intention, the path will reveal itself in time.

Rain, in all its forms, brings truths – some wash away the dust of denial, while others water the seeds of hidden pain. But always, they bring the clarity and growth necessary for healing.

The Weight of Awareness

The air of realization bears a heavy grief,
releasing the clasp on once-cherished beliefs,
and the haunting chorus of the 'would have', 'should be's.'

The Uncharted Self

Who were you before shadows of doubt
were cast?

What essence of you might have flourished,
unhindered by others' prescriptions on how to think, act, or feel?

Imagine a world
where we embrace every nook and cranny
of our beautiful beings,
unburdened by the fear of judgment—
what richness would that bring?

And in being unapologetically ourselves,
whose love might we risk—
and might that be the price
of our authenticity?

Enough as I Am

Hey, it's me—Jack.

I can do it all,
But it's not enough.

To be a master of none—

Who's to say
what I should master
and become?

I can do it all, but it's not enough...

For them.
But 'they', are not us.

Because, for some of us,
We have already won.

You are more than enough.

I am the author of my narritive,
my story is my strength.

Each day, I am learning to celebrate myself,
my journey, and the power within me.

In the tapestry of our journey,
each thread is a story,
a step,
a choice
that is uniquely ours.

We've been woven with enough vibrance
to stand alone,
yet we often find ourselves
measured against the hues
of others' expectations.

Remember,
we are already complete
in our mosaic of triumphs and trials,
more than enough
in our patchwork of passion and perseverance.

Let not the shadows of hurtful opinions dull the sheen of your fabric. They are as out of place as shoes on a fish—unnecessary, cumbersome, dragging down **what is meant to soar.**

In the depths of your being, know that the only validation you need is the pulse of your own conviction and the rhythm of your heart that knows your **true** worth.

Stand tall in your story,
embrace the power of your existence,
and extend a hand of understanding.

For when we see each other
not as unfinished sketches,
but as complete masterpieces,
we make room for a world
where every heart beats
to the rhythm of acceptance,
and every soul knows
it is,
    was,
       and
         will
           always
             be
              enough.

*We are all works of art in our own right,
complete and sufficient as we are.*

Touchpoint of Calm:
Anchored in the Storm

In moments when life feels overwhelming, grounding ourselves can offer much-needed stability. This touchpoint invites you to find your anchor amidst the tempest of challenges.

Ground Yourself:
If possible, stand or sit with your feet touching the floor. Close your eyes and take three deep breaths, focusing solely on the sensation of air filling your lungs and the steady beat of your heart.

Visualize:
Imagine standing resilient in a gentle rain, where each droplet represents the hurdles you've encountered. Visualize these raindrops nourishing the soil at your feet, sprouting into a lush garden around you. Each plant symbolizes a strength you've cultivated or a lesson learned from facing adversity. This garden thrives because of the rain, just as you grow stronger with every challenge you meet.

Through this visualization, recognize your inherent strength and resilience. Remember, it is within your power to thrive, no matter the storm.

Strength originates from within,
and no physical ailment can diminish
the immense power housed in your mind.

There are many who wear
their pasts like chains,
Allowing bygone days
to dictate their today.

They let themselves be buried
beneath old pains,
When it's the past that should
be laid to rest and fade away.

Regardless of the nature
of your relationship
with your parents,

We all had a mother;
We all had a father.

Yet, there comes a time in our lives
When we must learn to parent ourselves.

Our parents did the best they could
With the tools they had,
Even if some of those tools were broken.

*Our parents did the best they could
with the tools they had,
even if some of those tools were broken.*

Unwelcomed
Swept Away

My body is a guesthouse, each sensation a visitor, footsteps of pain, joy, sorrow, and delight leaving their imprint upon the doormat.

Some guests are courteous, pausing to wipe their feet, mindful of the space they enter. Others rush through, leaving behind muddy tracks, unaware of the care it takes to maintain a home.

Yet, regardless of their manners, they come and go—these fleeting tenants of flesh and bone. Oblivious to the fact that, with the changing seasons, comes a time for renewal.

And so, with spring's gentle touch, a thorough cleansing begins. Each corner aired, every surface dusted, all that is unwelcomed is swept out the door.

Like spring's renewal, I cleanse my spirit, welcoming growth and bidding farewell to what no longer serves me.

My body, resilient and tender, stands ready to embrace the next arrival with discerning grace. Its halls whisper with the silent strength of a sanctuary that, while always open, reserves its deepest warmth for the guests who come bearing the currency of kindness.

Here, love is not scattered at the feet of the unwary passerby but bestowed like a rare gift to those who step softly, who touch gently, who recognize the sacred ground they tread upon.

"When it rains, it pours," they say. But I like to think of it as nature's way of nudging us to dance more, love more, umbrellas optional.

Or, at the very least, to remember where we left that overpriced raincoat we vowed to wear.

When life gives you rainy days,
remember, ducks enjoy them.

Just watch out for puddles.

In moments of turbulence,
I channel the soothing essence of chamomile
and the tranquil spirit of lavender.

You are worthy—
even when you stumble
into the depths of darkness.

The light will always
be waiting for you
on the other side.

Are you always in search of the light?

Remember, rain is powerful too.
Flowers cannot bloom — without watered roots.

I get it
but YOU
got this!

She went fishing
for answers
and found
herself.

Go easy on yourself:

Sometimes, the true change we need isn't in ourselves, but in realizing we don't always need to be in a constant season of changing.

// embrace enough
// redefine progress

Yes, it's okay to take a break
from trying to be more
than you are right now.

But remember,
before you attempt
to change yourself,
change out the lens
through which you see yourself.

Once you do, the rest will follow.

Break free from the internal violence of your mind.

You do not deserve to be imprisoned by your own tormented thoughts, those relentless judges condemning you to a life shadowed by despair. Each thought a chain, each doubt a lock, holding you captive in a dungeon of your own making.

Yet, in the depths of this darkness, a spark ignites—a realization that you hold the key. That moment of clarity, when you see the chains for what they are: illusions, not iron.

Rise above these chains; your spirit is not meant to languish in a world that mirrors death, but to thrive in the light of living. It is in this pivotal moment, this choice to embrace your inherent power, that the walls begin to crumble, and the chains fall away.

As you step out into the light, remember: you are not destined for the shadows. Your spirit, unchained and free, is meant to soar in the boundless sky, to thrive in the warmth of the sun.

In breaking free from the internal violence of your mind, you reclaim your life. You are no longer a prisoner of your thoughts but the architect of your destiny, building a future where your spirit thrives, unbounded and luminous.

I am not a prisoner of my thoughts.

I am free from the chains of doubt and fear.

*My spirit soars, and my heart embraces the
limitless possibilities of each new day.*

*I am the creator of my destiny, and I walk
forward with strength, courage, and unwavering
faith in my journey.*

There are blessings in the messes.

You never really fail.
You never stop learning.
You never stop healing.
You never stop growing.

You are still here,
because you belong.

Hand on heart,
feel your worth validated
through your heartbeat's song.

Hand on heart.
I feel my worth validated
through my heartbeat's song.

Don't give up.
There's always one more tune,
waiting to be sung.

Even the edge couldn't let me go.

My time will come.
But not today.

Please, do not take away the days that belong to you.

Do not surrender under despair.

You belong here.

You Are Not Your Sorrow,
Your Sorrow Is Not You

I know you think you want
to take away all your days,
for this pain to go away.
But remember, you are not your pain,
you are not the sorrow in your veins;
you are more.

You have so many good days yet to see,
and yes, some darker days sprinkled in too.
But you are more than your sorrow,
you are more than your pain.

You are your heart.
In every beat, you embody resilience,
in every cell, you are infused with the essence of love.

Don't let your suffering keep you from
seeing the real you—
the you that deserves to live life fully,
the you that deserves to shine.

You are not your sorrow.
Your sorrow is not you.

I belong here.
I belong here.
I belong here.
I belong here.
I belong here.
I belong here.
I belong here.

Touchpoint of Calm:
Symphony of Resilience

In the Concert of Existence:
Acknowledge the symphony of your life, where every note – your struggles and triumphs – weaves a melody of unwavering resilience. You are an indispensable part of this symphony, deserving of every chord of joy and harmony.

Affirm Your Worth:
In the midst of life's tempests and showers, remind yourself, "I am grounded, resilient, and ever-evolving. I breathe in the strength to rise above challenges."

Embrace Your Worthiness:
Repeat three times, *"I was worthy then, I am worthy now, and I will always be worthy."* Let this mantra be a beacon through the storm, a reminder of your essential role in the symphony of existence.

This touch point serves as a reminder of your intrinsic worth and resilience. It's an invitation to see yourself as an essential note in the vast symphony of life, worthy of happiness and capable of rising through challenges.

You Are Worthy of Being Heard and Supported

In moments of doubt, know that seeking help is a testament to your resilience. *Your narrative is significant, and it deserves to be heard and supported.* Remember, you are not journeying in isolation but amidst a constellation of hearts and minds, poised to uplift and uphold you.

You are an irreplaceable thread in the tapestry of existence, never solitary, eternally significant. Caring specialists and compassionate individuals are within reach, waiting to stand with you as you navigate your path.

Consider this your gentle nudge, a whisper to seek out the guidance of those who stand ready to accompany you toward dawn's hopeful glow. Should you feel the need to reach out for support, **you'll find a haven on page 415**—a compendium of resources dedicated to supporting your continued journey.

Stand before the mirror, let each word **shatter doubts and limitations.**

Repeat them until they become your undeniable truth.

You are worthy of a life that blossoms fiercely, tearing down the walls that once confined you.

"I am a wellspring of strength, unyielding and vast."

"I am the architect of my peace, building bridges over my past."

"I am a mosaic of resilience, beautifully whole in every aspect."

Let these affirmations be your mantra, your shield against the world's noise. Each phrase is a testament to your inner power and unlimited capacity for growth and transformation. Like a chant, let them remind you of **your extraordinary essence.**

Life's storms cannot dim the light of your worth.
You are a beacon of strength, deserving of love and peace.

Remember, after the darkest night, the sun always rises.

In case no one has told you lately:

I am proud of you,
And you should be too.
Thank you for being here,
For courageously seeing another day through.

Checklist:
How to Find Strength in Storms

o   **Acknowledge Your Growth:** Recognize that, like rain nourishes the earth, each challenge you encounter fosters growth and strength within you.

o   **Discover Inner Solace:** Find comfort in your inherent resilience, an indomitable fortress standing tall against the tempests of life.

o   **Embrace Renewal:** See each downpour as a cleansing force, sweeping away doubts and illuminating your path with clarity and purpose.

o   **Seek the Silver Lining:** In the midst of a storm, search for the small moments of beauty or insight that can emerge. These silver linings can provide a sense of hope and direction during difficult times.

– Pen, Ponder, or Pass –
Embracing the Storm

Unexpected Strength: Reflect on a moment of unexpected resilience or strength during a difficult period. What surprised you about your response to this challenge?

Ideal Rainy Day Imaginings: Picture an ideal rainy day. What emotions and activities does it encompass for you?

Strategies for Peace: Identify a strategy or mindset that helps you find peace and comfort in challenging situations. How has this approach shaped your journey through difficult times?

Emotional Anchors: Recall a time when a specific person, place, or memory provided you with stability during a turbulent period. How did this emotional anchor help you navigate the storm, and what does it symbolize for you now?

Pour Me Love

Infusing the Heart with Sweet Aromas and Delicate Emotions

It starts with a shared laugh
and ends with a lifetime of memories.

Love, even in its wilting and ending, leaves behind a lingering fragrance, a lasting aroma that whispers to the soul of cherished moments and the beauty that once was.

Find gratitude in the rarity of love's unique fragrance, for some will never know such a scent.

Love is the only thing
that has the power
to hurt and heal,
to bleed and cleanse,
to embrace
and let go.

What lingering fragrance has a past love left in your life,
and how do you find gratitude in its memory?

Love's Dual Nature

Love possesses an uncanny duality, a two-sided coin of the heart that can both scar and mend. Like the gentle touch of a summer breeze that can unexpectedly turn into a tempest, love can caress us with its tenderness and, in the same breath, sting with its trials.

Have you ever felt the embrace of love so deep that it aches? A connection so profound that it permeates every cell, every thought, every dream. It's an exhilarating, almost surreal feeling, where you're lifted to the highest peaks of joy. Yet, this very same force can make the heart feel fragile, capable of shattering at the slightest tremor of doubt or misunderstanding.

But, in its enigmatic wisdom, love also carries the salve for these wounds. It's in the quiet moments of reconciliation, the shared tears, and the mutual understanding that we find its healing touch.

Just as it has the power to make us bleed, it also holds the magic to cleanse and renew.

Embrace love's duality:
where there is depth,
there is height;
where there is pain,
there is healing.

.

The Space Between

In that delicate balance,
between grasp and release,
where fingers linger and heartbeats sync,
there breathes a silent sanctuary.

A realm where love, understanding,
and emotions intertwine—
bestowing upon the soul
a profound stroke of solace.

// lovers hug

In every shared glance,
a promise of hope was sown,
and in a mere blink of an eye,
seeds of love
quietly sprouted
toward the sun.

// seedlings of affection

Touchpoint of Calm:
Essence of Connection

Embrace Togetherness:
Take a deep breath, allowing the enriching essence of love and connection to fill your being.

Visualize Unity:
Picture two hands intertwined, a powerful symbol of connection, trust, and unity. Let this image remind you of the strength found in togetherness and the beauty of shared paths.

*This touchpoint is designed to remind you of
the profound connections that enrich our lives.*

*It invites you to breathe deeply into the experience of love,
visualizing the tangible symbols of trust and unity
that bind us to one another.*

How has love transformed your perspectives, values, or priorities?

My love for you
is like the leaves
in autumn's embrace:

Capricious in hue,
dancing in the wind of joy
and under skies of gray.

Descending softly to the earth,
they rest and decompose.

Yet in this end,
a promise — for from the earth,
new life grows.

I tried to finish writing my story without you and ended with a blank page.

// blank page

I crave seeing the darkest parts of you,
so that I can shine my light on them.

Reveal to me the coldest parts too,
and I'll envelop them in a blanket of love,
like a cozy cocoon.

If my love were the sea,
its gentle tides
would guide you to tranquility.

If my love were a garden,
it would tenderly feed
your deepest roots with devotion.

If my love were the cosmos,
its stars would light your darkest nights –
embracing you until dawn's promising glow.

When his fingers whispered across the curve of my neck, a dormant passion awoke as if my soul was tasting desire for the first time.

Half-lit flames
are destined to fade
into embers.

Settle not for a love
that merely flickers
in the shadows
of half-heartedness.

Seek a love
that blazes fiercely,
one that burns
through every barrier,
igniting your heart
with an unquenchable fire.

The moment our hands touched
I knew that every dawn to dusk
was meant to be spent with you.

I find it captivating
the way your eyes sparkle
when you speak
so highly of the mountains,
and how your smile tilts
like the slopes
from your last ascent.

In these moments,
you reveal to me
the joy
held deep within
the crevices
of nature's heart.

I tried to write a million reasons
why I shouldn't love you...

And wrote a million reasons of why I do.

// rich off your love

I still remember the moment,
the first time our thighs touched.
We were so close
that your breath
became my breath.

It was almost as if my soul
left my body
for the first time,
only to greet the person
it called home.

When my soul returned to me,
it came back with a gift:
seeds of love
to bury in the garden
of my heart.

That's what love is.

My love for you
will not eclipse at the end of time.
It will transcend, beyond every twist and bend.
It will travel to the moon and beyond.
It will weather any storm.
It will always, always,
find you again.

My favorite song is the tune of your love.

- *my heart beats for you*

Your devotion to me,
holds my hand
in such a reassuring way.
Guiding me across bridges,
I never thought I could sway.

The Art of Devotion

In the quiet spaces between us,
there's a shared laughter that resonates,
like best friends conspiring in mischief.

His care is a gentle current,
cradling me in understanding,
a refuge in a world of complexity.

And amidst the grand tapestry of life,
it's the smallest strokes of kindness
that shine brightly.
His insistence on holding bags,
the courtesy of opening doors,
and never rushing ahead.

These are the brushstrokes of appreciation
in the portrait of us.

To me, you are more
than just a fleeting presence;
you are a dynamic,
ever-changing world,
rich with potential and mystery.

In your eyes,
I see galaxies yet unexplored,
and in your smile,
I find the warmth of a thousand suns.

You are, in every sense,
a world unto yourself—
irreplaceable, incomparable,
and infinitely fascinating.

What if we saw ourselves through the eyes of those who love us, basking in the light of unfiltered admiration and acceptance?

Your love blossomed
within me,
seeping gently
through my rugged roots,
and gracefully emerging
in my once dormant blooms.

I am transformed,
no longer the same
in essence or hue,
now radiant,
eternally altered
by the tender love
and affection from you.

In our garden of love, where our roots entwine and deepen over time, we find a foundation of unwavering strength and stability, nurtured by the sustenance of mutual care, enriched by shared experiences, and sustained by unending devotion to growth within ourselves.

I am Woman,
Delicate, yet hardy,
Soft, yet unyieldingly strong.

I possess the power
to birth new life into this world,
And cradle it tenderly in my arms.

Though my nails may grow brittle,
My heart wears an armor so fierce,
it's invincible.

You can't deny the indomitable force
of a woman's gentle strength.

I am a reservoir of grace and resilience,
nurturing myself with the same care I give to the world.

To truly love a wildflower,
you need to have strong roots,
a willingness to grow,
and a commitment
to nurturing your garden
above all else.

He said,
"You are a dream come true.
I never knew I could find someone like you."

I said,
"You never had to find me.
I've been with you all along."

// soulmates

Much like a flower,
love endures even when all its blooms
have gracefully kissed the earth
and a harsh frost looms on the horizon.

Trust is the gentle guide
escorting us to the awaiting season,
while hope boldly proclaims new life
with spring's tender awakening,
welcoming a cascade of bountiful hues.

Some seasons of love are bountiful as the midst of spring, where butterflies sing their cherished lullabies, and we're reminded of the earth's vibrant canvas, every color it can bring.

Other seasons of love resemble fall's embrace, shedding habits like leaves from an oak, yet remaining as steadfast as its trunk. Welcoming change as it comes, letting go with grace.

Some seasons mirror summer's radiant delight, full of playful days and nights so bright, a dance of life, in each moment, we ignite.

Then there are colder months, like bitter Midwest days in the middle of December, when we struggle to find our way, yet, we persist, though distant in various ways.

Through every season, even the harshest one of all, I want to love you with a steadfast call, for seasons change, but love stands tall.

In the game of love,
sometimes we're the poets,
at other times, the muse.

But most of the time,
we're just looking for the remote
while trying not to break each other's noses.

I want to build a house
for love to grow.

Dear love,

My house is not your guesthouse,
My heart is your home.
A refuge from the tempest,
Where you're never alone.

The walls are painted with our memories,
The windows reflect your glow,
Every corner echoes laughter,
And the tickles of warmth we've come to know.

The foundation's built on trust,
The beams on endless care,
Every room holds secrets,
Of intimate moments we chose to share.

Our garden blooms with passion,
Fed by rains of joy and strife,
Each season brings its changes,
Yet, our bond thrives in life.

So, my love, whenever you feel weary,
Know this truth to be shown,
My heart's not just a dwelling,
It's a place you will always know.

Tomorrow is never promised.
But I am happy
as long as I get to spend
my todays with you.

This relationship may be hard at times.
But you are easy to love.

Your silence
pierces the eardrums
of my heart.

I once thought
I could afford
the price of your love,
but no amount of money
can buy back trust.

We rushed,
driven by a lust
that f
    l
      o
        wed
through my veins,
yet it lasted only a moment,
a fleeting high – it was insane.

Now,
standing in the aftermath,
I see the true cost:
chasing such a drug
leaves a void,
deeply drained,
and lost.

Love's addictive allure,
this pain is a bust,
I'm weaning myself
off the drug of us.

// affection's antidote

Be careful whom you let walk through your garden.
If a petal drops with each touch instead of blooming with life,
then they have no business near your roots.

You are worthy of a partner who truly sees you,
who understands and accepts you for who you are.

You deserve more
than someone who exacerbates
your anxieties or past traumas,
especially intentionally.

'Good enough' often isn't
when it comes to matters of the heart
and choosing a life partner.

Life's challenges are enough on their own;
a partner who adds to that difficulty,
rather than easing it,
may not be the right one for you.

There is solace in recognizing
that it's never too late
to reclaim your power.

It's time to prioritize what you need
to be happy, safe, and at ease.

This is more than self-care;
it's self-respect.

Embracing the truth is the first step
towards a future where your well-being
and peace of mind are paramount.

Dearest, my love, my once-believed only,

The day we met was radiant and shimmering, like a scene from a fairytale. It was as if time held its breath. In that silent space, my body tingled in an enchanting way, as though I had been granted the momentary ability to feel what sparkles felt like. Your presence seemed to echo every whispered wish, every midnight dream I'd ever conjured.

But, as time unfurled its tale, reality began to chip away at the gloss. The dream began to blur, and I realized that love isn't a checklist of perfect moments or the embodiment of an ideal. True love is a journey, sometimes flawed, often surprising, but always real.

The fantasy man I once thought I saw in you was just that — a mirage of my making. And in recognizing that, I understood that love is more profound, more textured than any fantasy could encapsulate.

Even the brightest sparkles may fizzle out, but true affection is not just about the shimmer.

It's in the moments of darkness, in the clarity of real connection, where love reveals its authentic form.

Love's intensity
can sometimes
be overwhelming,
clouding judgment.

The journey of love
is not always smooth;
there are bumps, detours,
and challenges.

Before you consider going back:

Remember, not all relationships need to be a rollercoaster of push and pull, highs and lows, or constant triggers.

Safe, stable partners do exist.

While no relationship is without its conflicts and trials, genuinely nourishing and supportive partnerships are possible. They bring growth and comfort, rather than constant upheaval.

Don't settle.

Hold out for a connection that nurtures and respects you, one that adds to your life without bringing needless drama.

**You deserve a love that feels like home,
not a battleground.**

Words that embrace your heart:

Comfort
Nurture
Harmony
Affection
Gentleness
Serenity
Compassion
Warmth
Empathy
Tenderness

You have walked
the path of love,
felt its highs,
and braved its lows.

But even amidst
the ache of loss,
you've felt love's
deepest touch,
life's most profound
form of affection,
despite the sprinkles
of its woes.

Forever bonding,
transcendent,
beautiful and so
rarely experienced.

So, for those who've
felt love's embrace,
for those who've loved
and been loved in return,
remember, life's most
precious echo
will transcend forever
within your heart
and in your soul.

Nurturing self-love alters how you perceive and accept love from others. It naturally diminishes undue expectations and eases the process of letting go of what no longer serves you.

In loving yourself, you find the balance to enrich others' lives without depleting your own.

Filling your own cup isn't about being self-centered or selfish; it's about understanding that you are as deserving of deep, meaningful love as anyone else.

When you prioritize self-love, you enhance your capacity to both offer and welcome love, creating a cycle of genuine, fulfilling connections.

Let me ease your worries:

You made the right decision in not chasing.

You've done the best you could, in every way that counts.

Yes, you are enough – more than enough.

If they couldn't see your worth, remember,
it's not a reflection of you, but of their current state in life.

Your true value remains, shining bright,
unchanged and undiminished, in spite of their oversight.

Self-love goals:

Cultivate a relationship with yourself so robust that you understand: people who enter your life aren't there to fill a void. They're there to complement an already rich and fulfilling existence.

Think of them like the rolls served at a restaurant – delightful to have, certainly adding to the experience. But essential? Well, that's debatable.

You're perfectly capable of enjoying the main course of life on your own. These 'extras' should enhance, not define, your dining experience.

Your life is a feast in itself.

In this garden of life,
you will meet countless faces.
You will face a myriad of challenges
in various places.

But when you turn inward
and face yourself with grace,

You'll sprout the seeds of freedom,
cultivating a newfound blossoming space.

For what it's worth:

Now, you carry a ledger of lessons learned,
each obstacle faced a chapter of its own.

You've experienced heartbreak, but through it, you've also discovered
the resilience of your own heart, and the depth of your capacity to
love and be loved anew.

You've had to say goodbye, but in those farewells, you've reclaimed
pieces of your identity, learning the empowering art of letting go and
the grace of moving forward.

You've known failure, yet each misstep has been a stepping stone to
wisdom, teaching you the value of persistence and the beauty of new
beginnings.

For every shadow cast in your path, there's been a light of insight,
guiding you to a richer understanding of life, of yourself.

How can the calming qualities of chamomile and lavender inspire you to cultivate a more loving and peaceful relationship with yourself and others?

You cannot love your neighbors
as yourself...

until you love yourself
as yourself.

Uniquely You

You are like a bouquet
of freshly picked flowers,
glistening under the gentle touch
of morning dew.

Each petal, each scent,
crafted just for you
and only you.

In a garden full of blooms,
yours is a melody
sung in its own tune.

So embrace your individuality,
let your beauty unfurl
and bloom.

Even when your hair is a mess,
you still look your best,
because the best look
on you
is you.

// perfectly flawed

In the expansive canvas of the world, we often admire the iconic masterpieces, the epitomes of beauty as defined by society. Yet, in the unassuming alcoves, far from the gleaming lights, the true essence of human spirit flourishes. It's in the laughter lines that map our joys, the scars that narrate our battles, and the messy hair that dances freely to life's rhythm.

True beauty isn't found in the immaculate or the idealized; it resides in the genuine, unedited snapshots of our existence. It's in embracing the disarray, the unpredictability, and even the flaws that we uncover the most genuine representation of ourselves.

So next time you glimpse your reflection, with disheveled hair or amidst a chaotic day, remember, it's these perfectly imperfect instances that craft your distinctive masterpiece.

You are going to be the best thing,
that has ever happened to somebody.

"I love you"

- *my reflection*

In what ways have you been your own support system recently?

We take pride in being a safe haven for others, and rightly so.

It's an admirable feat to cultivate an environment where authenticity and vulnerability can thrive.

But what about you?

Have you mirrored that same care within,
crafting an oasis of love and understanding for yourself?

You, too, deserve a sanctuary where your true self is nurtured.

It's time to extend that same compassion inward,
to build a refuge in your heart where you can rest,
be unguarded, and truly at peace.

In doing so, you honor not just others, but yourself too.

My pledge to self:

I pledge to view my flaws as facets of my beauty,
embracing each quirk as a brushstroke in my life's portrait.

I vow to treat my needs with reverence, never to sideline them,
acknowledging that nurturing myself is as vital as breathing.

I commit to pouring into myself the energy I give to the world,
recognizing my worth and the love I deserve.

I promise to celebrate every step forward, big or small,
and to greet setbacks as lessons, not as failures.

I will cultivate my inner garden with patience and care,
giving myself the grace to blossom at my own pace.

I vow to be my strongest ally, my most understanding friend,
affirming myself with the same compassion I share with others.

*In embracing these promises, I embark on a path of profound self-love,
understanding that the way I treat myself resonates throughout my existence, shaping every interaction and every moment of my journey.*

Checklist:
Cultivating the Garden of the Heart:
Love's Nurturing Steps

o   **Water the Roots of Your Relationships:** Trust and nurturing communication form the foundation for growth. Regularly invest in these aspects to ensure a strong and healthy connection.

o   **Clear Away the Weeds:** Misunderstandings and resentments can suffocate the potential for growth. Make it a practice to address and clear these barriers, allowing for new understanding to blossom.

o   **Admire Every Small Gesture:** The smallest acts of love and care are the petals that beautify your relationship. Recognize and cherish these moments for the joy they bring to your heart's garden.

o   **Prioritize Self-Love:** The soil from which all forms of love grow is self-love. Cultivate this core with kindness and understanding, as it is essential for the health and vibrancy of all relationships.

– Pen, Ponder, or Pass –
Reflections of Love

Profound Touch: Reflect on a moment when love profoundly touched your heart. What emotions did it stir, and how did it change your perspective on love?

Test of Strength: Describe an experience where love tested your strength and resilience. How did you grow from this challenge, and what did it teach you about the nature of love?

Unexpected Joy: Share a memory where love brought unexpected joy, comfort, or clarity to your life. How did this experience enhance your appreciation for the small, yet significant, moments of love?

Love's Quiet Presence: Think about a time when love was expressed not through words, but through actions or simply being present. How did this quiet expression of love impact you, and what does it teach you about the unspoken ways love can manifest?

Pour Me Healing in Sorrow

Brewing Healing in the Soil of Sorrow
Crafting Infusions of Memories and Blends of Comfort

In the silent garden of grief, we often find ourselves wandering, seeking solace amid the shadows of what once was.

This journey, although unique for each traveler, treads universal paths—be it the deep ache of a loved one gone, the melancholy of dreams faded, the pang of a self once known, or the sorrow of relinquishing a relationship that no longer nourishes our spirit.

But, in this quiet sanctuary, as we confront our sorrows, we also unearth the treasures of empathy, strength, and wisdom. Like a gardener tenderly caring for a withered plant, our hearts learn to nurture moments of joy and hope, sprouting amidst the tears.

So, while grief may momentarily dim our world, it's in this very darkness that we learn to light our inner lanterns, guiding us to a horizon where pain meets grace, and endings bloom into new beginnings.

As you journey through these pages, I invite you to reflect on your own experiences of grief in its many forms.

Giving Grief a Voice

It's time for you to give grief a voice.
Let it scream through the silent corners of your battered heart.

Let your wounds drip from your lips
and taste the sorrow that haunts you.

For too long, suppression has been welcome at your doorstep,
but now, you get to face what this pain has to say.

Today is the day you pave the path to being okay.

What pain have I been suppressing, and how can you begin to express it safely?

When you left,
My face glistened like
Dew drops dripping from
The velvety leaf of a mullein.

Loss can make you feel isolated, as if you're speaking a language only you understand.

Comfort: But through this journey, you'll find others who speak your language, who understand, and who can walk alongside you in empathy and understanding.

Dismantling the Walls of Grief

You've carefully unpacked your sorrows, constructing a home where pain is the foundation.

This abode, lacking a back door, keeps you enclosed with your lingering grief. Here, the relentless rain of sorrow falls, with no gutters to redirect its course, pooling into a stagnant reservoir of unexpressed emotions.

Within these walls, you've become the sole occupant of a house built from heartache.

The **tools in your hands**, once wielded to seal yourself away, **now hold the potential for your emancipation.**

It's time to let the light penetrate the gloom, to tear down these barriers not to forget the past, but to embrace a future of healing and openness.

Begin the work of dismantling these walls, not to erase what was, but to **open a pathway** to what can be. Each strike against the brick and mortar of your sorrow is a step towards a renewed self, where fresh air replaces the stale echoes of the past, and the open sky beckons with hope and new possibilities.

When your world
weeps tears of pain
from the cloud
eclipsing the sun,
allow your sorrows
to be cradled
by the tender embrace
of the wind.

I never used to value sleep the way I do now. Before, I would say,
"You'll have plenty of time to sleep when you're dead."
But now, I've discovered a newfound appreciation for my night's rest.

For in my dreams, you are there—
the only place I can feel your greatest presence,
the only place I truly feel like me.

// cherished dreams

Somber Hues

As I gazed upwards, the world seemed enveloped in a thick, relent-less haze. The usual brilliance of the skies was absent, the colors of the day appeared muted, and the vivacity of life felt subdued. Such a scene took me back to that fateful time—when you took your last ascent.

This day, bathed in somber shades, was unlike any I had ever wit-nessed. Gloom permeated every corner, as if the universe itself was mourning with us. A profound sadness hung tangibly in the air, as though a piece of our collective soul had taken flight, seeking you amidst the vastness above.

// universe in grief
// muted horizons
// grief's colors

The world feels a little bit colder
without your warm smile.

Time moves like sludge when you're grieving.
When it's hot, it speeds up, granting brief relief.
When cold, it halts, frozen still.
And often, you're stuck
in that in-between chill.

Touchpoint of Calm:
Starlight Remembrance

Gaze into the Cosmos:
When the night is clear, allow yourself a moment under the stars. Let each twinkling light represent a cherished memory, a deep bond, or a moment of profound love, forever shining in the sanctuary of your heart.

Embrace the Warmth of Connection:
Connect each star to a treasured memory, allowing the warmth of those connections to envelop you, offering celestial comfort that bridges time and space. This warmth is a gentle reminder of love's undying light and the everlasting comfort it brings, even in absence.

Engaging in this act of stargazing serves not only as a tribute to lost loves but as a tangible connection to them, through the timeless beauty of the night sky.

It's a moment to cherish the enduring nature of love and the memories that, like stars, illuminate our darkest nights sky.

I can't move on without you.
I won't move on without you.

- *I will*

Acceptance is not the end
but the beginning
of finding peace
within the storm.

How do you navigate the balance between honoring your grief and seeking joy in life?

There are days when the weight of grief becomes too much to bear, when the shadows cast by our pain darken every corner of our existence. It's almost as if we resist letting the light creep in through the blinds of our sorrow, stuck in a place where moving forward feels impossible.

Yet, we must remember that there is no right or wrong way to grieve, and **we equally deserve moments of respite from our pain.**

In these times, it's essential to recognize the need for a gentle pause.

Imagine cradling your grief, folding it with care, and placing it within a serene box, just for a while. This act is not about forgetting, betraying, or diminishing the love you hold; it's about allowing yourself a moment to breathe, to find a moment of peace,
even as grief relentlessly ferments around you.

Silence is the loudest form of pain.
It's the ache that has nothing left to say,
a wound buried so deep within,
that even if it could speak,
no one would be there to truly understand.

In my moments of sorrow, I am gentle with myself,
understanding that healing is not linear.

Remember, it's okay to give yourself moments of respite from grief.

Love, after all, is not tethered to the constant presence of sorrow.
It exists in every quiet heartbeat, in each cherished memory, and in
the echoes of shared laughter.

Our love for those we've lost transcends the bounds of grief;
it is an immortal flame within us.

In these pauses, we honor our lost ones not with perpetual sadness,
but through the enduring vibrancy of our love for them.

As we step back into life, they accompany us, not as shadows of grief,
but as beacons of love and resilience that guide us forward.

The rain's serenade whispers a gentle reminder:
it's okay to embrace stillness,
to cradle your sorrow,
to mourn, and to be enveloped in solitude.

For even the bluest of skies sometimes
take a moment to express their somber tunes,
crafting a symphony that heals,
harbors hope and renews.

I allow myself to feel, to mourn,
and to let tears flow,
knowing that it's okay to not feel okay.

"These memories
hurt so good."

- *my heart*

Grief is like an unending ocean,
with waves that sometimes calm
but never fully cease,
a heart that continues to ache,
and a story echoing silently within.

But in welcoming healing,
you open the door to new beginnings,
allowing fresh tides of life to wash ashore.

Scatter the ashes of the old you.
Grieve for the person you once were,
and embrace the new.

Grief of self, while raging within the confines of our soul, is a silent humbling storm.

We grieve for the person we were, for the life we thought we'd lead. Yet, it is in this grieving that a transformation begins. Slowly, we wipe away the tears, the layers of a persona that no longer serves us, and start to uncover whispers of our true essence. These whispers grow louder, guiding us back, not to who we were, but to who we are meant to be.

As we scatter the ashes of our old selves, a new journey begins. It's a path lit by the flickering flame of self-discovery, revealing truths we never knew existed. This path might be uncharted, but it resonates with an authenticity we've never felt before.

It's here, in the shedding of the old and the embracing of the new, that we find ourselves again – not as we were, but as we truly are, ready to step into a future unburdened by the ghosts of a self that no longer exists.

Chamomile & Lavender:
A Gentle Embrace

In the quiet hours, when grief feels like an unending night, consider a simple ritual of solace: brewing a cup of chamomile and lavender tea. Let the soothing aroma be a gentle reminder of nature's embrace. As the warm cup rests in your hands, let each sip be a small act of self-care, a moment to reflect and breathe.

Chamomile, with its calming essence, mirrors the peace we seek, while lavender's subtle strength embodies the resilience within us.

In this ritual, find a momentary respite from your aches. Let the tea be a companion in your solitude, a quiet acknowledgment of your pain, and a soft whisper of comfort.

Remember, in the blend of chamomile and lavender, there's a reflection of life itself—a balance of tranquility and enduring spirit.

They keep hurting me
And I keep letting them
They
Is
Me

"I don't love you anymore,"
she whispered,
gazing into her reflection,
a moment
of painful introspection.

With a wave of compassion,
she began to
w
  i
p
  e
a
w
a
  y
the
tear-streaked
highways of mascara
gracefully from her cheek,
pondering how she had lost herself,
how she had strayed so far
from the woman she vowed
to never leave behind.

In the labyrinth of life, where paths often twist unexpectedly, we sometimes find ourselves at a crossroads, holding the fragments of a self we no longer recognize. The plans we meticulously laid out, the dreams we thought were our destiny, can unravel, leaving us stranded in a landscape of unfamiliar desires and uncharted aspirations. In these moments, we confront a profound sense of loss—the mourning of a self that once was, a phantom of our own making.

It's in this space, amidst the echoes of a life we meticulously scripted but no longer fits, that we feel most lost. We have everything we thought we wanted, yet we grasp at the air, feeling empty.

Like sand, our old identity slips through our fingers, and we stand, gazing at our own reflection, a stranger staring back with eyes full of questions.

Who is this person?
Where did the dreams of yesterday go?

I am still in the process
of shedding parts of me
that I no longer know.

Yet, through this journey
of self-discovery and healing,
I remain steadfast
in my determination
to become whole.

Let the tears that soften your soil
under the sorrowful sky
plant seeds of hope and rebirth,
as you come back alive.

// nourishing tears
// emotional revival

Grief: a dance with the eye of a storm. Rooted in moments of calm amidst chaos. Never knowing when your world will feel the weight of the loss crashing in.

The thought of you
is immortal,
consuming me,
devouring
my budding hope
upon the horizon.

Just as I am starting to see the light,
your shadow casts its darkening cape,
and once more,
I am thrown
into the unfathomable depths
of you.

Grief has a way of trespassing through the walls of a perfectly good day.

They say, 'Grief is love with nowhere to go,'
yet within every hollow of my being,
it's found a place to grow.

In every pulse,
in every beat of my ever-bruising heart,
through each alternating thought,
it never departs.

It consumes,
defines,
and becomes all of me—
yet still, I grapple with understanding
who 'me' is anymore.

I believed I'd moved past it,
As the pain no longer spoke.
But in the quiet, it dawned on me,
Numbness is just another cloak.

I thought
I would
See
You
One
Last
Time.

I dreamt of one more laugh,
One more tear shed in unity,
One more song,
One more dance,
One more apology,
One last embrace.

But now, all that remains is the thought of you,
Moments I wish I'd held onto longer,
Hugged a bit tighter,
Sang a touch louder,
Apologized when it mattered,
Danced until our feet could bear no more.

This period of mourning you're enduring is the unfortunate price of profound love.

We cannot feel the depths of such pain without having journeyed through the rich valleys of love.

Words that comfort the soul:

Solace
Peace
Consolation
Relief
Tranquility
Compassion
Mercy
Support
Understanding
Healing

Touchpoint of Calm:
Memory Lane

Reflect:
Think back to a joyful time spent with someone you miss. Let this memory be a soft light, casting warmth over the shadows of your sorrow.

Visualize:
See yourself reliving that special day—the sounds, the laughter, the comfort. Let the vividness of this memory wrap around you like a comforting blanket, soothing your grief and rekindling joy within your heart.

Navigating the Tides

This journey is a silent voyage
without a captain,
an unpredictable path
seemingly at the mercy of the tides,
where waves of sorrow
wash over the present,
engulfing moments
with their depth.

Yet, in time,
despite these sporadic storms,
the tide will calm.
The ship, once adrift,
shall find its course,
propelled by the healing breezes
of love and hope.

In what ways has grief deepened your empathy, compassion, or understanding?

Losing you
is like the phantom pain
of a severed limb,
an ache that lingers,
a void that's hard to dim.

Your absence echoes,
a haunting reminder
of the love we once shared,
words of comfort
I will never hear,
and advice
that was sometimes
hard to bear.

Woven into
these fragile memories,
though the threads
continue to tear,
your essence remains intact,
a presence
I will forever hold dear.

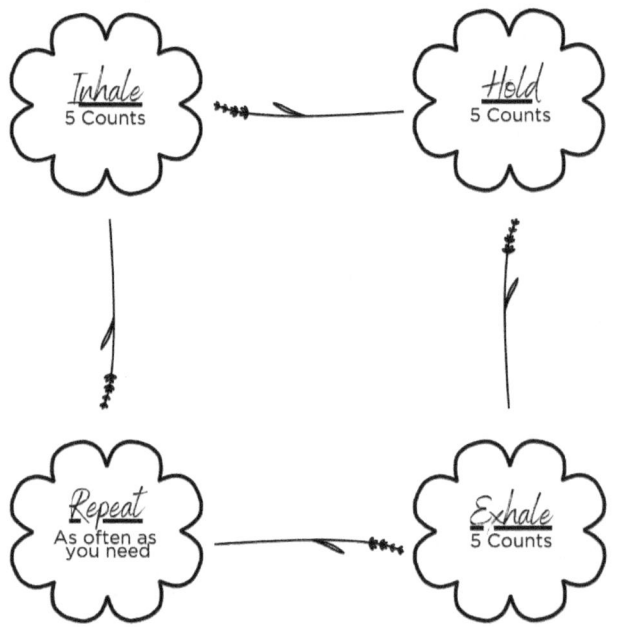

I still have that cozy lavender blanket you gifted me on that unpleasantly cold December night. I remember the way your face lit up when you handed it to me, the joy in your eyes knowing it was in my favorite color. You'd be delighted to know I've wrapped it around me every night since.

Yet, with each passing day, the weight of its love seems to fade, as if each thread is slowly losing its memory of you. Season by season, it grows lighter in my hands, its once comforting embrace becoming more of a whisper than a hold. I fear one morning I'll wake up to find it reduced to just a few feathers and a ball of strands.

Where did its comfort go?
Where is the warmth?
I do not understand.

His laughter,
a vibrant cadence
— now silent —

Vibrates the eardrums
of my heart;
a melody once felt,

Too deeply to forget,
Too dearly to let go.

Alas, his presence
— a song without sound —
lingers in the quiet.

Memories
of you
are like
grains
of sand
in my hand,
slipping away with time.
Yet they momentarily slow,
clumping up
from the tears caught
from my eyes.
Relentlessly,
I grasp
for those moments
as they crumble
through
my
f
i
n
g
e
r
tips.

It's in those moments of quiet

that I miss you the most.

When my heart beats

and I don't hear yours

echo back at me.

// broken echo

You were my first thought.

- *my last breath*

He never truly departed;
his essence still lingers
in every nuanced crevice of my life.

He is more than the hollow
I've made his home;
he is a constant, palpable presence.
In every silent thrill,
every fleeting moment,
he's there—undeniably here.

Beyond the space
where our hearts once met,
in every tear shed
and hill of regret,
he remains.

He is the subtle hum
in the depth of my emotions,
the indelible mark
in my journey of memories
and moments.

He is undeniably here.

// enduring imprint

Love transcends time and physical presence, remaining alive in the deepest chambers of our hearts and in the essence of those we've loved.

Grieving is a journey through the nature of the soul, where each fallen petal becomes a memory, and every tear creates a sea of love.

Words to hold close in grief:

Compassion
Presence
Comfort
Memory
Courage
Solitude
Healing
Acceptance
Hope
Peace
Release
Renewal
Recovery
Remembrance

When I look at myself in the mirror,
I see you in my eyes.
And that makes
me happy.

Though I grieve,
I also carry within me the unbreakable legacy of love
and memories shared.

Touchpoint of Calm:
Reflection in Water

Visualize:
Stand before a calm lake at dawn, its surface reflecting the sky like a perfect mirror. Gaze into the gentle ripples and see the reflections of your loved one.

Feel:
Allow the peace of the scene to resonate within you, a reminder of your loved one's enduring presence in your life, symbolized by the persistent ripples on the water.

This touchpoint is intended to provide a moment of serene reflection, emphasizing the continuing impact of loved ones in our lives, mirrored in the natural beauty around us.

It's not just about moving on from your grief, nor is it about finding ways to live without them. It's more about embracing the gift they left inside you, and how their essence can still play a significant part in your life. Their presence now takes a different form, but it remains deeply ingrained.

Find ways to cherish and honor them, to weave their memory into the fabric of your everyday life. If they loved sunflowers, sew a sunflower patch on your coziest blanket. If baseball games were their joy, make a tradition of watching a game every year on their birthday. If the mountains called to them, go for a hike in their memory. Wherever you go, whatever you do, their spirit can be a guiding light in your journey.

In every action
that honors their memory,
they live on.

Their love, their laughter, their very essence finds new life through you. So, when you find yourself amidst sunflowers, at a baseball game, or on a mountain trail, remember: they are there, not just in memory, but in the very act of living that honors them.

Embrace this transformed presence, for in these moments, you are not just recalling them — you are keeping their spirit vibrantly alive.

You are undoubtedly strong.
But just because you can handle pain and abuse
doesn't mean you should.

Grieving for someone who is still alive,
yet no longer present in the way you need,
can be a profoundly disorienting experience.

It's a unique form of loss,
one where the person you counted on
to be there for you
seems to slip away before your eyes.

The emptiness that you see in their gaze,
once filled with warmth and understanding,
now mirrors the void they leave in your heart.

Every Grief is Valid:
Embracing Healing from Unseen Losses

It may seem mindless to compare the grief of those with a beating heart to those that have departed, but this kind of grief is a silent torment, marked by the haunting presence of what was once a source of comfort and security.

It's not just about missing someone; it's about mourning the loss of what you shared, the betrayal of expectations, and the dreams that now lay fragmented at your feet. Each piece a reminder of a future that will never come to pass, and a relationship that has irrevocably changed.

Yet, in the heart of this silent grief, remember that within you lies an enduring strength, a light that continues to shine even in the shadow of lost connections. This light guides you towards healing, reminding you that you are whole, capable of finding peace and forging new paths of joy and fulfillment.

// healing in the quiet

The release of relationships that dim our light is not loss but liberation, paving the way for a journey back home to our true essence.

Reflect on a moment when trust was broken, and the grief that followed. How has this experience of loss and betrayal shaped your understanding of forgiveness and self-growth?

Our trauma whispers warnings, urging us not to trust, and I hear you. The sharp sting of betrayal, realizing those once trusted can no longer be relied upon, is like a boat losing its anchor amid a storm. Adrift and disoriented, you find yourself swept into dark, turbulent waters, engulfed by a profound sense of loss and confusion.

In this tempest, where betrayal and abandonment threaten to over-whelm, the descent into despair seems inevitable. Yet, it's in this soli-tude that a crucial realization dawns: the path to salvation lies within. Embracing the power within your pain, you discover the resilience to remain buoyant. This resilience, your beacon in the tempest, guides you, showing that amidst chaos, your spirit is indomitable.

By acknowledging this inner strength, you begin to navigate the stormy seas with newfound determination. The journey through grief is arduous, but within you lies the capacity to heal, to rebuild trust in yourself and, eventually, in others.

Remember when he choked me

and pinned me against the wall?

Remember when I called out for you,

and you did nothing at all.

You Always Have Someone To Call

In the shadow of grief and betrayal, the feeling of solitude can be overwhelming. It's a part of mourning, not just for people or dreams lost, but for the life you once pictured.

Yet, in this solitude, hope remains. Support is closer than you might think. The resources on page 416, along with local help, are ready to offer comfort and guidance.

Remember, your strength surpasses the pain you face now. Each step toward healing is a journey back to your inner resilience. Don't hesitate to seek out the support you need and deserve. As you make your way forward, remember that I'm here, supporting you in spirit.

You always have a place to turn,
and a hand to hold.

Sometimes, forgiveness blooms not from the deafening apologies of those who wounded us, nor from the words we yearn to hear.

True healing and forgiveness instead unfurl from the strength rooted in the silent musings of our own hearts, like flowers opening to the first light of dawn after a week of cloudy days.

// create your own light
// heal your own heart

In the dim chambers of memories past,
there lies a pain, not born of your own doing.
A shadow, unjustly cast by another,
dims the brilliance of your heart.

How dare they tarnish
something so inherently beautiful and pure?

Yet, remember this:
the world is vast and filled with wonders.
You are deserving of every radiant hue,
every gentle breeze, every tranquil moment.

Do not let the wounds of betrayal
anchor you to a time and place
where joy is obscured.

**Do not grant your oppressor the power to linger,
to darken each sunrise,
to silence the songbird's serenade.**

Healing takes time, yes.
The path is not a straight line
but a winding journey of introspection and discovery.

But trust that,
with each step you take,
even when it feels like retracing old grounds,
you are moving towards
embracing the world's beauty once more.

Sometimes, grief can make you question the very purpose of existence, shaking the foundations of your beliefs.

Comfort: Yet, it is in these moments of questioning that we often find our deepest truths and forge a stronger connection with ourselves and the world.

I trust that my struggles are guiding me
to profound truths and inner peace.

I am still learning
who I am
without you here.

Missing you in moments yet to unfold,
picturing you in a future that now will never be.

// absent tomorrows

I long to experience love for life again,
but since you've left,
I've forgotten how to love at all.

'They' say you should
love yourself first anyway,
but how can I,
with this gaping hole in my chest,
where my heart used to rest?

You've ruined me.

Before you left,
with you by my side,
I felt like I was always
my Sunday best,
as if I had it all.

And now,
I'm left
with nothing.

// after you left

I am worthy of love and healing,
even in my moments of deepest pain.

Each day,
I take a step towards rediscovering the love within me,
knowing that I am whole and complete on my own.

Maintain your garden
with kindness and devotion,
and butterflies will come.

Perhaps your garden remains barren, not for lack of seeds,
but because its roots thirst for more.

It's your soul that needs nourishing, and your passions that crave
watering.

Remember, gardens bloom not just from the soil they're in,
but from the care they receive.

Start doing what you love, and watch your garden sprout radiant
hues.

// self-care harvest

What is one act of self-kindness you can offer yourself?

You still deserve to heal
from the things keeping you up at night.

// restful healing

*I trust in my ability to rebuild and find love within myself
and the world around me.*

Grief might dim the lights,
but memories of shared laughs
have a way of sneaking in
and flipping the switch,
briefly waking us back up again.

// flickers of joy

For those with loved ones
on the other side,
remember, within you,
they will always reside.

Share their memories,
spread their love,
for it continues,
forever and always,
in your heart's tender cove.

Let the light in,
for the world
has so much love
left to offer you.

Like a flower
after a harsh winter,
you too have the strength
to shed your wilting petals,
to rise from the cold ground,
and to bloom anew
in all your splendid glory.

If love can truly heal,

then here,

take a piece of my heart.

// healing heart
// shared strength

Checklist:
Navigating Grief with Compassion

o   **Embrace Your Feelings:** Recognize and allow yourself to experience the full spectrum of your emotions. Whether it's sadness, anger, confusion, or even moments of joy, understand that all these feelings are valid parts of your grieving process.

o   **Seek Supportive Spaces:** Connect with people who offer comfort and understanding. Whether it's friends, family, support groups, or professional counseling, find safe spaces where you can express your grief and feel heard.

o   **Create Moments of Remembrance:** Honor the memory of your loved one in ways that feel meaningful to you. This could be through writing, creating art, visiting special places, or sharing stories about them.

o   **Practice Self-Care and Compassion:** Prioritize activities that nurture your well-being. This can include simple acts like taking walks, reading, meditating, or engaging in hobbies that bring you peace. Remember, caring for yourself is not a betrayal of your grief, but a necessary part of healing.

– Pen, Ponder, or Pass –
Reflecting Through Grief

Moments of Memory: Reflect on a cherished memory that brings you comfort. What feelings does this memory evoke, and how does it help you feel connected to what you've lost?

Expressions of Emotion: Grief can manifest in various emotions. Write about an emotion you've experienced deeply during this time. What has this emotion taught you about yourself and your capacity to heal?

Finding Solace: Identify something that has brought you solace in your grief. It could be a place, an activity, or an object. Describe its significance and the comfort it provides.

Steps Toward Healing: Consider one small step you can take to-wards healing today. It might be as simple as going for a walk, calling a friend, or writing in your journal.

Pour Me Midday Clarity

Blending Moments of Respite and Insightful Reflections

In the full swell of the day, the energy of life radiates with vivid intensity. Celebrating silence for the first time since dawn's intrusion, I clasp my chamomile and lavender tea. It's crystalline and comforting, serving as an anchor against the day's unrelenting current.

I pause, allowing myself to bask in the myriad wonders that stitch the fabric of my existence: threads of bygone tales and monumental marvels.

Yet, amidst this quiet contemplation, the jarring jangle of a spam call slices through—an absurd interjection. Like ripples disturbing my peaceful pond, it stands as a stark and bizarre contrast to the otherwise symphonic rhythm of my surroundings...

What a peculiar world we live in.

Is midday a time of reflection or anticipation for you?

No matter how out of tune the day's rhythm might be,
love's subtle notes always play in the background.

Gently swaying in the weathered hammock,
I'm swaddled by the robins' midday song.

Their melodies are a vibrant echo of endurance,
testaments declared through each note and chirp,
telling a story of survival.

This composition is a reminder:
find gratitude in simplicity,
cherish life's fleeting chances,
and embrace the promise of regeneration
that each new day brings.

Amid the day's stillness, I contemplate: am I nurturing my plants with care; or am I submerging their dreams beneath the tide of my overzealous attentions?

Words that inspire midday reflection:

Pause
Ponder
Breathe
Reflect
Center
Stillness
Quietude
Calm
Respite
Meditate

Touchpoint of Calm:
Quiet in the Crowd

Reflect:
Pause to appreciate how even in the busiest environments, we can carve out moments of solitude and reflection.

Visualize:
Picture a vibrant square teeming with activity, where everyone is engrossed in their daily routines. Amidst this scene, envision a person sitting on a bench, calmly observing the world around them. They are at peace, untouched by the chaos, finding their personal oasis of quiet.

This visualization serves as a reminder that peace can always be found—not by escaping the world, but by finding a way to exist peacefully within it.

When noon casts its boldest shadow, I ponder life's tiny wonders: the delicate aroma of my tea, the way light filters through my curtains; and the ever-present *enigma of missing socks...*

I am grateful for this moment, the gentle pause in my day that allows me to ponder and appreciate the world around me.

Steal a slice of serenity
amid the day's relentless pace—
a tranquil enclave crafted
by your own blueprint.

It's the perfect moment
to ponder the unpredictable,
perplexing moods of printers
and to silently hope
that you remembered to hit 'mute'
on today's Zoom call.

Have you made friends with your darkness?

We must not shun our darkness.

It's all too easy to crave temporary light, to force a bloom in a season meant for hibernation, all for the comfort and approval of others. Yet, this contradicts our very essence. Never let anyone dim your shine, and certainly, don't mask your true self to fit into someone else's narrative.

We must learn to embrace our vulnerabilities, to move through our emotions with compassion and courage.

It's about building a support system within ourselves.

If you need to weep, let your tears form a river, carry you away to confront the deepest, most haunting parts of your being. It's in these depths, in the heart of your personal forest, where you'll find the most profound strength and understanding.

This journey is not about seeking external validation or comfort.

It's about discovering the resilience and solace that resides within you. In facing our inner darkness, we find not only acceptance but also the courage to be authentically, unapologetically ourselves.

If I need to weep,
I will let my tears form a river.

I will allow them to carry me to confront the deepest,
most haunting parts of my being.

In this vulnerability,
I find my true strength and understanding.

Why do hearts ache for the stray dog,
lost and alone on the street?

Yet, for the homeless person beside,
empathy skips
a beat.

It's time to redefine our interactions.

To answer 'How are you?' with genuine feelings and to ask the same with sincere intent to listen.

We need to do better at being there for each other, at recognizing the silent pleas hidden in half-hearted responses.

A hurt heart can indeed be held by a friendly smile, a simple gesture that says, 'I see you, I hear you.'

Our smiles, those windows through which our compassion shines, have the power to uplift, to heal, to connect.

In helping our neighbors, in showing love through the simple act of smiling, we do more than brighten their day; we lighten their emotional load.

This is a call to peel back the layers of our guarded hearts, to reach out and touch another soul with the authenticity of our own experiences.

It's a reminder that in being present for others,
we also heal parts of ourselves.

Ode to the Highways

Highways weave accessible paths to the world's wonders.

Each state harbors its unique treasures:
Artifacts from eras past, distinct languages, mannerisms cast.

From rolling plains to towering peaks,
to fields that offer the nourishing crops we seek.

Let us show gratitude to the stars for these vast highways.
They let us traverse to distant zones, embrace a friend, and feel their
very bones.

To dance with kin at joyful reunions,
and bid farewell to the departed under mournful suns.

Some view them as sources of decay,
scarring our already tarnished sphere.

Yet, it's these roads that draw our loved ones near.

*Sometimes, it's the unnoticed that deserves our deepest gratitude—
for in the everyday, we find life's profound magnitude.*

At the end of the day,
it is what it is,
a tapestry of moments,
woven with threads of reality and wish.

It will be what it will be,
a journey unfurling unexpectedly,
navigating through calm and stormy seas,
an adventure crafted from life's vast,
boundless mystery.

And you, resilient spirit, pure and free,
are everything you will ever need,
a galaxy of dreams, emotions, thoughts in a sacred creed.
Embracing yourself, constantly, ever-evolving,
and sowing self-love's seed.

If you're worrying about tomorrow,
then let's wait for it to come.
Let's focus on today
and what is yet to be done.

Live in the moment,
under the radiant sun,
for in the present,
a new journey has just begun.

As the sun
reaches its radiant peak,
I take a moment
to reflect.

Life's intricate dance
is a bit like brewing tea—
sometimes it's the burn
of the midday sun
that truly brings out
the flavor.

And sometimes,
I just wonder
if the sun feels
as overworked as I do.

It is okay
to take a day
to be
and let be.

Midday has arrived,
and you feel time slipping away,
wondering, '*What have I even achieved today?*'

But then you see, against all odds,
you woke up; you showed up.

You tackled yesterday's woes,
with hope nestled firmly between your toes.

You greeted today,
a feat not all know.

And now,
the hardest part is already behind.

So do your best,
and let life's path take care of the rest.

Remember,
you've got this!

Not every day needs to be your Sunday best.

Tonight,
let's have you leave
the clothes in the dryer,
the dishes in the sink.

No need to take a shower,even if you stink.

You see what's important for today
is to take some time to sleep,
to ease,
and to be.

You've done so much for others,
and not enough for yourself;
you work and work,
and give and give.

But please,
for today,
just live.

*Just as the sun warms the earth,
I warm the hearts of those I reach with my glowing
acts of love.*

In the soft embrace of a Sunday afternoon, there I was cocooned on the porch, cradling a poetry book close to my heart, like a mother holding her firstborn.

The agitated hum of the neighbor's lawnmower and the playful dashes of their yapping dogs came together, creating a unique symphony of life's simple moments.

Amidst this familiar jangle, a profound serenity enveloped me, heightened only as I took a bite of my sandwich. Its layers were generously, some may even say excessively, smeared with peanut butter — my soul's first true love.

Each bite brought bits of comfort I so desperately sought that day.

As I delved into the verses of my cherished poetry book, a particular passage reached out to me. Feeding my spirit in ways no peanut butter ever could. With each ingested word it gently unraveled the pain I had hidden away, dissolving its deep-seated roots with a tender touch.

This literary embrace transformed my outlook,
infusing me with hope and offering a respite from my sorrows.

In that poignant moment, the cleanest corner of my napkin became a bookmark, a modest yet powerful testament to poetry's nourishing embrace and the pure, simple joys that ground us. It marked where optimism was rekindled, ensuring I could always return to this sanctuary of comfort again.

// poetry heals

In waiting for the perfect poem,
You silence the words that need to be heard.

For those who seek solace in your voice,
May never find the comfort they deserve.

Consider this...

Maybe you are more than you give yourself credit for.

Perhaps what you perceive as mistakes are actually highways leading you to the right way.

Imagine each misstep not as a detour, but as a vital part of your journey, guiding you towards wisdom and growth.

Maybe the moments you thought were failures were, in truth, stepping stones, paving your path to where you need to be.

In every choice, in every turn you took, there was learning, there was meaning.

Consider that you are exactly where you are meant to be, not in spite of your past, but because of it.

Thieves of Joy:
The Illusion of More

True fulfillment is never nestled in the bag of jewels you seek.
It eludes us when the weight of our wants overshadows the
gratitude we hold for what we already possess.

In this imbalance, we unwittingly become our own thieves of joy,
pilfering from the most precious treasure we have: the gift of the
present moment, the truest gem of all.

Writing my way back home to you.

- Self

It's okay to cut that PB&J in half.

And lick that ice cream off the spoon, too.

And next time you see that swing at the playground,

you know what to do.

// echoes of a younger, freer sky

Wave at your neighbors,
Hum with the bees,
Sing with the birds,
Dance with the trees.

Dress up like the butterflies,
In the colors that suit you best.
Show up for yourself often,
And don't forget to rest.

I go to the forest
not to escape,
but to belong.

Most days, I'm like a star
masked by a thick and cloudy throng,
yearning for a moment,
a chance to shine bright and strong.

As I drift through life,
seeking where I might fit along,
in the forest, I connect,
a dance to nature's lifelong song.

Amidst the towering trees
and the babbling brook's gong,
I am grounded, I am whole,
here is where I am drawn.

I go to the forest
not to escape,
but to belong.

You can't be behind or ahead
if you are on your own path.

You are where you are.
And that's okay.

Each step you take,
every choice you make,
unfolds a new path,
revealing opportunities
previously unseen.

While the journey may be riddled
with challenges and uncertainties,
remember that the vast expanse
also offers countless moments
of joy, learning, and growth.

Embrace the voyage with an open heart,
for within this realm,
you have the power to shape your destiny
and create a tapestry of experiences
uniquely your own.

Touchpoint of Calm:
Your Unique Journey

Pause for Reflection:
In the midst of your day, find a moment of stillness. Close your eyes and take deep, measured breaths. With each inhalation, gather peace; with each exhalation, release comparison and doubt.

Contemplate Your Path:
Reflect on your journey's distinct rhythm—its highs and lows, its pace, and its direction. Embrace the truth that there's no "behind" or "ahead" on a path that's uniquely yours.

Simple Affirmation:
Gently affirm to yourself, "My path is mine alone; I am exactly where I need to be." Let this thought fill you with a sense of calm and belonging.

Let this touchpoint be a reminder:
your path is a personal narrative, rich with its own stories and mile-stones, deserving of recognition and respect.

In the brief lull between meetings and messages, I found a minute for solidarity, as rare and precious as silence in the crux of New York City.

It was enough to remind me—who I am beyond the perpetual rush.

On boundaries: a journey within

Often, when we talk about boundaries, our minds turn to the limits we set with others. These are undoubtedly crucial, but there's a deeper layer we must explore: the boundaries we set with ourselves. It's easy to blame others for overstepping, **but if we consistently find ourselves tolerating more than we should**, it's time for introspection.

This pattern of allowance is a form of **self-neglect**. It signals a need to delve into our relationship with ourselves.

Are we truly honoring our heart, spirit, and inner child? If we're enduring more than we'd ever want for someone we love, we're not.

This isn't solely about others crossing our boundaries; **it's about understanding why we let them.**

Often, people will continue to cross lines if they know they can, sometimes subconsciously, sometimes with a hidden motive.

Perhaps their actions serve as a warning, a sign pointing us towards areas within ourselves that need healing. Parts of us that, for too long, have believed we deserve less than we truly do.

It's a journey of self-discovery and healing, learning to assert our worth and to listen to our inner voice that knows what we truly deserve.

Setting boundaries with oneself is the first step in respecting and loving who we are, paving the way for healthier relationships with others and, most importantly, with ourselves.

The path to self-discovery is never a straight line;
in each detour, there's a lesson,
in every bend, an opportunity to grow.

Embrace every twist and turn.

// whirlwind of possibilities

Touchpoint of Calm:
Embrace the Now

Breathe:
Inhale deeply, drawing in the present moment with all its nuances and textures.

Exhale:
Release any pressures or expectations that weigh you down. Let them flow out with each breath, leaving you lighter.

Savor:
Relish this moment of peace. Recognize the value of simply being here, now, without the need to rush forward.

This touchpoint is designed to remind you of the power of pausing in the midst of a hectic day, offering a space to recalibrate and appreciate the immediate experience, away from the rapid pace of daily tasks and achievements.

Medicine for your mind:

- Water your mind as diligently as you water your plants –
  and really do it.

- Make walking a part of your routine, a journey for both
  body and mind.

- Speak affirmations; let them be your daily mantras of
  strength and positivity.

- Stop scrolling.
      Yes, you, stop scrolling.
          Once more, stop scrolling.

- Throw open your blinds, let the sunlight cascade in, bathing
  your space in warmth and light.

- Read something – a book, a blog, a poem. Nourish your
  mind with knowledge and inspiration.

- Eat well, as if your life depends on it – because, in many
  ways, it does.

- Meditate. Take deep breaths. Try box breathing or any form
  that resonates with you.
  But most importantly, breathe with intention
  and awareness.

*Let these mind medicine rituals be your anchor, grounding you in
the present, where peace and clarity flourish.*

Who you were,

Who you are,

And who you will become.

  ... notes in the beautiful song of "You."

Every achievement,
no matter how small,
is a milestone on your journey.

Honor them all.

You,
like evolution,
are nature's elegant design;
your capacity to shift, mold, and flourish
is in perfect harmony with the universe's eternal melody.

...I still can't find my other sock

But...

You've come so far.

Celebration is found not only
in the thundering triumphs
but also within the subtle,
fleeting moments
that are easily
misplaced.

Remember,
it's in these gentle pauses and reflections that you can feel
life's intricate texture within the palm of your hands.

Checklist:
<u>Cultivating Serenity in the Daily Rush</u>

- o **Celebrate a Morning Achievement:** Reflect on the morning's achievements, no matter how small, and acknowledge your progress.

- o **Embrace a Brief Respite:** In the midst of busyness, find a short moment for tranquility—close your eyes, breathe deeply, and center yourself.

- o **Reframe a Current Challenge:** Use the clarity of midday to gain fresh insights into any challenges, opening doors to new solutions and understanding.

- o **Allow Your Mind to Wander:** It's okay to let your mind wander and ponder. Give yourself permission to think freely and see where your thoughts take you. This mental journey can be a source of unexpected joy and creative solutions. Enjoy the ride.

– Pen, Ponder, or Pass –
Midday Reflections: Moments of Clarity

Insightful Revelation: When has a revelation in the middle of your day unexpectedly shifted your perspective? Explore this insight and its impact on your day.

Oases of Calm: In the rush of daily tasks, how do you carve out oases of calm? Reflect on the rituals or moments that bring you respite.

Small Joys: Recall a recent small joy that brightened your day. What was it, and why did it bring you happiness? Is this a moment to cherish, or does it inspire a change in your daily routine?

Midday Gratitude: What is something or someone you are grateful for today? Reflect on how this feeling of gratitude shapes your outlook for the rest of the day.

Pour Me Peace into the Closing Day

Steeping in the Peace and Wisdom of the Setting Sun

Evening's serenity is all about perspective. Sometimes I see a poetic sunset, other times I see a night off from watering the plants.

This is the hour of pouring peace into the closing day, where every exhale is a release of what no longer serves us, and every inhale is an embrace of the present moment and an acceptance of who we are today.

It's in this sacred transition that we find comfort, not in the endless pursuit of what might be or the heavy chains of what was, but in the rich, vibrant reality of now.

Letting go and embracing the now means accepting who you are today, not who you expected yourself to be.

Not everyone who saw last night's moon got to greet the morning sun. Absorb the light you were graced with today with gratitude and purpose as you welcome the prelude to the night's sky.

She dwells in a realm
of self-awareness and mystery,
confident in her identity,
yet wandering in realms of the unknown.

Her days are a tapestry
of joyous laughter under the setting sun,
and nights, a solemn journey
of tears until the break of dawn.

Admired for her resilience,
a pillar for many,
her hidden sorrows, though,
often evoke a silent empathy.

In a dance of healing,
hurting, nurturing, and loving,
she sometimes feels anchored in place,
amidst life's relentless flowing.

She embodies a universe
of contradictions,
a blend of everything
and an echo of nothing.

In her is the coexistence
of fierce storms and serene skies,
a living paradox,
where profound depth and surface collide.

Grab a blanket and curl up in the coziest corner of your home.

As mother nature dims
the light for some evening ambiance.
Let your spirit *sway*
to the gentle rhythms
of chamomile
and lavender *whispers*.

// melt the day away

Our hands are made to hold on
But that doesn't mean they shouldn't let go.

The Sweet Symphony of Sunset

As the sun dips below the horizon, painting the sky with hues as sweet as cotton candy, a profound tranquility emerges in this daily spectacle. Sunset's gentle farewell is not just the close of a day; it is nature's poetic gesture, teaching us the art of letting go with the sweetness of beauty and grace.

Each sunset reminds us that endings, though inevitable, can be imbued with serenity and hope. It is a natural encouragement to find closure, to make peace with our past, and to face the uncertainties of the future. As the light softly fades, there's an invitation to embrace the calm of the evening, preparing us for the renewal ushered in by a new dawn.

In the quiet departure of the day, a message of hope and continuity whispers to us. It's an ode to the cycles of life, a gentle guide towards finding personal peace and resolution within the perpetual dance of endings and beginnings.

I left the old tattered welcome mat
out on the porch.

Though it kept falling apart
more and more
through each storm or windy day,

still, I could not throw it out.

I couldn't bear to part with it—
for there was love in every thread.

// love always returns home

Life brings us fleeting companionships,
like shadows cast by clouds on a sunny day,
constantly shifting and moving on.

Some things, some people,
drift into our lives only to leave again,
like a breeze that touches your skin
and then vanishes.

Their temporary stay,
a brief chapter in our story,
teaches us the art of cherishing
and then releasing.

In their departure,
we learn the poignant truth of transience
and find solace in the natural ebb and flow of existence.

Touchpoint of Calm:
Evening Release

Visualize:
Imagine standing by a gently flowing river under the soft light of the moon. The water moves steadily, carrying leaves and small branches downstream. Envision yourself holding a small, glowing orb in your hands, representing your worries and burdens from the day.

Feel:
The coolness of the evening air fills your lungs as you take a deep breath. The gentle flow of the river mirrors your breath, in and out, calm and steady. Feel the weight of the orb in your hands, acknowledging the stress and concerns it represents.

Release:
Slowly open your hands and let the glowing orb float away on the surface of the river. Watch as the current carries it downstream, gradually fading into the distance. With each breath, feel a sense of lightness and relief, as if the river is washing away your burdens.

Embrace:
Embrace the freedom that comes with letting go. Allow the peaceful rhythm of the river to soothe your mind and heart. With each inhale, draw in the serenity of the night, and with each exhale, release any remaining tension. Let this moment of detachment bring you a deep sense of peace and renewal, preparing you for a restful night ahead.

What if every fear
that whispers doubts in the night
was met with the courage of a thousand sunrises,
burning away the shadows of uncertainty?

What if each tear shed
was a pearl of wisdom,
a precious testament to our journey
through the seas of life?

Be Bold

Be bold,
Even when others try to dim your light,
When they cast shadows on your brightest days.

Be bold,
Even if it feels like the timing's not right,
When the world tells you to wait.

Remember, comfort isn't always found
On the well-trodden paths of old.

True growth lies in the steps untaken,
In the stories yet to be told.

It's time to chart a new course,
To venture beyond the familiar.

Take a leap, make your mark,
In the canvas of life, be a vivid color.

Be bold,
For in boldness, you'll find
The strength to redefine,
To reshape, to renew –
To be unapologetically you.

I hear you, and it's time:

You've been wronged, deeply and unfairly.
This pain was never meant to be yours to carry.
But now stands before you a pivotal choice,
to rise, collect the pieces, and find your voice.

These fragments,
sharp and scattered at your feet,
bear the marks of your journey, bitter yet sweet.
Your resilience, your love for self, are the keys
to piece them back, to set your spirit free.

Healing, though a path rugged and steep,
is a responsibility that's yours to keep.
It won't be easy, this journey to reclaim,
but it's time to start, in your name.

Your story isn't over,
it's just begun to turn,
towards a chapter where you heal,
you grow, you learn.

So, embrace this call, let your heart align.
I hear you, it's tough, **but trust me – it's time.**

Words that help you let go:

Release
Forgiveness
Closure
Liberation
Surrender
Detachment
Tranquility
Easing
Unburdening
Acceptance

Sometimes we have to accept
that letting someone go
is the best way we can show
them that we love them.

Evening Mantra

As the day softly fades,
I embrace peace,
releasing thoughts and burdens
that no longer contribute to my well-being.
These elements begin their final journey
as they flow through me,
dissipating beneath my feet into the earth.

Rooted in the depth of my inner strength,
I perceive each departure not as a loss,
but as a natural progression.

This strength reshapes my view of farewells,
transforming them into opportunities
for growth and new beginnings.

In this cycle of letting go and moving forward,
I find my true peace,
harmoniously aligned
with life's continuous evolution.

The moment I sit down
with my warm cup of tea,
I just know everything will be alright.

The herbs infuse my soul
with hope and reassurance,
melting away the troubles of the day.

Each sip is a soothing balm,
a gentle reminder that amidst life's chaos,
there are pockets of peace
where everything falls into place.

Love,

You've just navigated a major shift, and it's completely normal to feel a bit adrift, barely skimming the surface of stability. Rest assured, you made the right choice. Now, it's about giving yourself the time to acclimate to this new chapter of your life.

Grant yourself some grace during this transition. It's okay not to have everything figured out immediately. With time, you'll find your footing, and everything will begin to fall into place.

Trust in this process and in the journey you've embarked upon.

How do you rejuvenate and reset after significant closures?

When Wealthy Men Beg: The Wisdom of the Poor

Imagine if more people grasped the real essence of being rich. It's not found in the weight of your wallet, but in the depth of your love, the joy of pursuing what your heart yearns for, and the fulfillment that comes from living with purpose and intention.

Such true richness is profoundly compelling, to the point where it could even make the wealthiest yearn for the treasures held by the 'poor.'

Tonight, as you welcome the night sky,
take a moment to breathe in the nourishing air
gifted by the trees.

Thank the moon for the tides it brings,
and the sun for the life it breeds.

Express your appreciation for the gentle breeze
that whispers secrets of the world to the leaves.

Close your eyes, and in gratitude,
let nature's symphony sing you to sleep.

One exceptionally cloudy day
during my brisk morning walk,
I slowed to capture a precious moment
between an elderly gentleman who stood tall
on the front of his porch.

He was looking intently at his rosebush,
and the rosebush graciously looked back at him.
Locked into a silent exchange,
I couldn't help but wonder
what was going through his mind
as he gazed into the eyes of the last seven blooms.

Did he see reflections of himself in the wilting beauty?

Was he quietly contemplating life's fleeting moments?

Perhaps mourning the blossoms that had departed to the other side,
or cherishing the precious few that still remained?

My heart concluded,
in that intimate moment,
man and nature shared a secret understanding,
a mutual reflection on the fragility and resilience of life.

Ageless Wisdom:
A Journey of Understanding

I used to be afraid
of people of old age back then.
Being young and full of life,
I felt like a stranger to them.
With their gray skin and wrinkles,
I just did not understand.

Especially Grandmother Julia -
she was old, frail, and thin.

They compared me to her frequently,
which just didn't make sense.
The only thing I knew for sure
is that we were kin.

But now, I greet that time of life
with gratitude and anticipation,
so grateful for the many moons and suns
that I have seen risen.

Through the years of aging chapters,
I have found many lessons.
Each line, a tale of growth,
in its own unique expressions.

No longer a lone stranger,
but a traveler on the same road.
In their company,
life's fullness I've come to behold.

And with every passing year,
a new tale to tell,
I see you now, Grandmother Julia,
with your beautiful yellow skin -
wise and well.

What lessons have sunsets taught you about peace, acceptance, and transition?

As the rolling water
prepared to meet the leaves of the tea,
a tranquil duet
patiently awaited.

The gentle nature of chamomile,
paired with the dreamy essence of lavender,
sang a melody
of peace and comfort...

Touchpoint of Calm:
Moonlit Reflection

Visualize:
Imagine a quiet garden bathed in the soft glow of the moonlight. The flowers and trees are gently swaying in the night breeze, creating a dance of shadows and light. Envision yourself walking through this garden, feeling a deep connection with the tranquility around you.

Feel:
The cool touch of the night air on your skin, refreshing and calming. Let this sensation help you release any lingering worries or tensions from the day. Feel the ground beneath your feet, solid and supportive, grounding you in the present moment.

Embrace:
With each step, embrace the peace of the night. Take in the sounds of the evening—perhaps the distant hoot of an owl or the rustle of leaves. Let these sounds lull you into a state of relaxation. Reflect on the day's experiences with gratitude, knowing that you have the strength to face tomorrow with a calm and open heart.

You can't make it to the end by skipping chapters.

// embracing life's progression

We all end up at the same stoplight.

Within the vast mosaic of existence, where myriad paths weave together in intricate patterns, we journey forward. Each of us, a traveler with tales etched in our steps, bound by hopes, fears, joys, and regrets. Yet, as fate would have it, amidst the diversions and detours, we converge at a singular point.

A stoplight, where all narratives momentarily intertwine. Here, differences dissolve, and stories merge, reminding us of life's greatest irony. No matter the roads we tread or the speeds we adopt, we all await, in collective anticipation, the same signal to continue.

In this pause, we're united, if only for a heartbeat, by the universality of our shared existence – waiting for the light to guide our next step.

It's a reminder to cast a kind smile, extend a gesture of patience, for in this collective dance of life, it's not about who gets ahead, but about traveling with grace and understanding. For at its core, life isn't a race, but a montage of interconnected tales.

You can look back.

But please,
don't linger there.

*I embrace the peace and stillness
of life's gentle farewells.*

*Embracing endings allows me to cherish
new moments with deeper gratitude.*

Some journeys are meant to be walked alone.
Like leaves carried away
by an autumn breeze,
certain things in life
drift into their own paths,
paths where we cannot follow.

This parting,
though it may bring a tinge of sadness,
is a natural rhythm of life.
It teaches us that not everything we encounter
is ours to keep.

And in this understanding,
we find a gentle freedom,
a letting go that allows us
to appreciate the beauty
of things both present and departed.

Not everything is meant to be found.

Sincerely,

Sock

What if forgiveness was the path to your sunset?

I am the architect of my serenity,
building bridges of forgiveness and understanding
within my soul.

I release:

I release the weight of past mistakes, allowing myself to step into the light of forgiveness and move forward with grace.

I release the grip of worries about the future, embracing the present moment with trust and openness.

I release the barriers I've built around my heart, inviting in love and connection in their purest forms.

I release the need for perfection, recognizing the beauty and strength in my imperfections.

I release the fear of change, knowing that each ending is a promise of a new beginning.

Forgive yourself for:

Forgive yourself for the times you thought you weren't enough, for each dusk you spent doubting your worth under the fading light.

Forgive the promises to yourself you couldn't keep, and the expectations that fell like leaves in an autumnal sunset.

Forgive the reflections in the mirror that didn't smile back, and the harsh words you whispered to your own shadow.

As the day concludes its vibrant display, let go of the harsh judgments and the self-imposed limitations.

Embrace the tranquility of the evening, understanding that with each sunset comes an opportunity for renewal and forgiveness.

Allow yourself to bask in the soft, forgiving glow of twilight,
knowing that every nightfall is a gentle closure,
a quiet preparation for *"Pouring Peace into the Closing Day."*

Checklist:
How to Pour Peace into Closure

- ○ **Witness the Sunset:** Remember that all things have a graceful end. Let the sunset remind you of life's beautiful cycles.

- ○ **Release the Day's Burdens:** With the setting sun, allow your worries and stresses to fade into the horizon.

- ○ **Embrace Endings:** Understand that endings are essential for growth and renewal. They are a natural rhythm of life.

- ○ **Find Solace in Closure:** See closure not as an ending, but as the promising seed of tomorrow's bloom.

– Pen, Ponder, or Pass –
The Art of Letting Go

Embrace the Quietude: As the sun sets, casting amber hues across the sky, take a moment to reflect on the quiet moments of your day. What peace did you find in these moments, and how did they influence your overall sense of well-being?

Reflect on Release: Consider something you've been holding onto that no longer serves you. It could be a grudge, a worry, or a self-limiting belief. Write about what it would mean to let this go. How would releasing this weight alter your emotional or mental landscape?

Contemplate Forgiveness: Forgiveness can be a powerful tool for release and renewal. Think about a situation or individual you're ready to forgive, including yourself. What steps can you take to initiate this process of forgiveness? How does the idea of forgiveness impact your feelings towards tomorrow?

Letter to Your Younger Self: Inspired by the concept of "I release" found on page 408, take a moment to write a heartfelt letter to your younger self. In this letter, gently address any burdens, fears, or insecurities you're now ready to let go of. Extend words of encouragement, love, and hope for the journey ahead to your younger self. *Reflect on how this act of writing and consciously releasing impacts your view of the past and shapes your path forward.*

Concluding Note:
The Last Sip Letter

As we reach the final notes of our journey, standing at the precipice between sunset's gentle farewell and the awaiting dawn, this closing message is not merely an end but a passage to new beginnings. This book has been an odyssey through the heart's vast terrain, navigating between light and shadow, resilience and vulnerability, discovery and acceptance. The "Bitter Truths" served as beacons, guiding us through introspection's night with unwavering honesty. Through "Pen, Ponder, or Pass," we've mapped the soul's depths, unearthing hidden gems within our essence. The "How to Checklist" segments have been our compass, guiding us from the fog of uncertainty to clarity's shores.

This book was a chalice, filled with the elixir of life's essence. As the last words dissolve on your tongue, like the aftertaste of a rich tea, the journey's essence—its insights, emotions, and awakenings—remains with you, a guardian for the path ahead.

Pause here, in the beauty of ending and the thrill of what's next. Every word imbibed has sown seeds in your consciousness, ready to flourish. May you carry the courage from the bitter truths, find comfort in affirmations, and draw wisdom from reflective silences. Let the Touchpoints of Calm, marked by chamomile tea tabs, continue to guide you to moments of peace and reflection.

As we close this chapter, let us not talk of endings but of ongoing stories. Your narrative, now intertwined with "Chamomile and Lavender," will continue to unfold in wondrous and unforeseen ways. Greet each new day as a fresh chapter, ripe with potential and infused with the knowledge gained on this path.

With the final sip, may you feel the warmth of shared connection, the solace of collective growth, and the inspiring call to welcome each day with an open heart and an eager spirit.

Continued

As you linger over the last sip of this journey, take a moment to ponder:

❖ Which passages within these pages echoed most profoundly with your own experiences? Why do you think they stood out to you?

❖ Reflect on the themes of peace, comfort, and introspection woven through 'Chamomile and Lavender.' How have they brushed against the canvas of your life?

❖ Looking forward, how do you envision integrating the insights and lessons from 'Chamomile and Lavender' into the tapestry of your daily existence?

I look forward to sharing more moments of reflection and growth with you in the future.

With warmth and solidarity,

Sonesta Wilde

<u>Mental Health Resources Page</u>

When the Pages Pause and Life Persists

There are times when the comforting embrace of words must give way to the supportive hands of community and professionals. This book may journey with you through various stages of your emotions and experiences, but please remember: seeking help is a brave and vital step towards healing and growth.

If you or someone you know is in need of immediate support, these national resources offer confidential assistance from trained specialists. You are not alone, and help is available. Sometimes, the bravest thing we can do is reach out for support.

***

The following resources are for U.S. residents only but I encourage those out of the U.S. to seek resources near you.

<u>We all deserve to feel supported</u>
<u>and cared for.</u>

For a full list of resources, please refer to **Page 416.**

Resources List

- **988 Suicide & Crisis Lifeline:**
  - Call: 988
  - Online Chat: 988lifeline.org/chat

- **Crisis Text Line:**
  - Text: "HELLO" to 741741

- **The Trevor Project (for LGBTQ+ youth):**
  - Call: 1-866-488-7386
  - Text: "START" to 678678

- **SAMHSA's National Helpline (Substance Abuse and Mental Health Services Administration):**
  - Call: 1-800-662-HELP (4357)

- **National Domestic Violence Hotline:**
  - Call: 1-800-799-SAFE (7233)
  - Online Chat: thehotline.org

- **RAINN National Sexual Assault Hotline (Rape, Abuse & Incest National Network):**
  - Call: 1-800-656-HOPE (4673)
  - Online Chat: rainn.org

- **National Child Abuse Hotline:**
  - Call: 1-800-4-A-CHILD (1-800-422-4453)

- **Veterans Crisis Line:**
  - Call: 988 and press 1
  - Text: 838255

Remember, it's okay to not be okay.

It's okay to ask for help.

It's more than okay—it's a courageous step forward.

Tea Recipes for the Soul

The Alchemy of Tea:

In the quietest moments of reflection, tea has been my steadfast companion. Its gentle warmth and the deliberate act of preparation have often mirrored the very essence of healing, comfort, and the delicate unfolding of awareness. Just as each chapter of this book has offered a passage through the varied landscapes of emotion and experience, so too do these tea recipes intend to complement your journey. Crafted with intention, each blend is an olfactory and gustatory echo of the chapters you have just explored.

Allow these recipes to be more than a mere directive for brewing; let them be an invitation to cultivate presence, to savor each note, and to steep yourself in the essence of each moment.

May these teas be your silent conversants as you pause, reflect, and find peace within.

Brewing Notes:

Each tea recipe here is an allegory, a sensory counterpart to the emotional and spiritual terrain you've traversed in the preceding chapters. As you prepare each cup, do so with mindfulness. Boil the water, select your leaves or herbs, and watch as they release their essence into the water. Notice the colors, the aromas, and the steam rising in gentle spirals. Allow the act of making tea to be meditative, an extension of the calm and introspection fostered by your reading.

Consider the preparation of these teas as the final step in each chapter's journey—a ritual to anchor the lessons and insights you've gathered.

May each sip be a closing verse to the poetry of your experience, leaving you settled, soothed, and ever more connected to the depths of your own being.

Dawn's Awakening Blend

- Green tea leaves
- Orange peel, finely grated
- A hint of lemon verbena
- A sprinkle of dried cornflower petals

Preparation:

Steep the green tea with orange peel and lemon verbena in hot (not boiling) water for 2-3 minutes. Strain and garnish with cornflower petals.

This cup offers a gentle nudge to awaken with the new day, its citrus notes promising hope and zest for life.

Midday Clarity Elixir

- Peppermint leaves
- Fresh lemongrass, chopped
- Rose petals

Preparation:

Infuse peppermint leaves and lemongrass in freshly boiled water for 5 minutes. Add rose petals for the last minute of steeping for a hint of floral sweetness.

Ideal for a midday moment of clarity and rejuvenation,
this tea is a reminder to cherish the now.

Storm's Embrace

- Black tea
- Fresh ginger, thinly sliced
- Turmeric root, grated
- A touch of honey (optional)

Preparation:

Brew the black tea with ginger and turmeric for 4-5 minutes. Sweeten with honey if desired.

This potent blend is your anchor in the tumult, a warm embrace in the midst of life's storms.

Blossom's Heart Tea

- White tea leaves
- Dried jasmine flowers
- Hibiscus petals

Preparation:

Steep white tea and jasmine flowers in just-boiled water for 3-4 minutes, then add a sprinkling of hibiscus petals for a vibrant, heart-opening infusion.

Sip this to celebrate love's flowering in all its forms.

Serenity in Sorrow

- Chamomile flowers
- Valerian root
- A dash of lavender buds

Preparation:

Let chamomile and valerian root meld together in hot water for 7 minutes, adding lavender in the last 2 minutes for a calming aroma.

This brew is a companion in solace, a balm for the weeping soul.

Sunset's Repose

- Rooibos tea
- Cinnamon stick
- Anise star
- Orange zest

Preparation:

Brew rooibos with a cinnamon stick and anise star for 5 minutes, finishing with a twist of orange zest.

This is your cue to unwind, to bask in the day's last golden rays as evening beckons.

Acknowledgments

To my former partner and friend, Beau. Thank you for helping to pick me off the ground when I made darkness my home.

To Eli, the mountaineer soaring in the sky, the man who lived many lives while on this earth. You always knew I could become a writer someday. You will always have a home in the cove of my heart. Thank you for inspiring me in more ways than I could ever put into words. I promise to always try to live a life of purpose, compassion, and intention.

To my family and friends, to the strangers on the street, and to anyone who has crossed my path in this lifetime. You are all a part of my world in some way, and I wouldn't be the person I am without you. I will forever be grateful for that.

And to you, dear reader, friend, companion on this collective journey we call life. Thank you for your vulnerability, for being here, for being you.

I love you all so much.
And yes,
I love you, too.

Keeping in Touch

Thank you for joining me on this journey through *"Chamomile & Lavender: Sips of Peace, Comfort, and Introspection."* Our shared moments of reflection and growth mean the world to me, and I would love to continue this connection beyond the pages of this book.

Stay updated with my latest writings, thoughts, and inspirations by following me on social media or visiting my website. Simply **scan the QR code using your phone below** to connect with me on Instagram.

Website: www.sonestawilde.com

SONESTAWILDEPOETRY

Feel free to reach out, share your thoughts, personal stories, or just say hello.

I look forward to sharing more moments of peace, comfort, and introspection with you.

Let's keep this beautiful journey going together!

I love you

Who Even is Sonesta Wilde?

Sonesta Wilde is a unique fusion of tranquility and boldness, navigating the serene waters of poetic expression with grace and elegance. Her writing exudes a soft, calming ambiance, akin to a gentle breeze or a peaceful lakeside at dawn. Yet, she ventures beyond calm reflections, exploring life's deeper, intricate facets, finding beauty in both light and shadow.

Just when you think you've captured her essence, Sonesta surprises with a dash of wit or a playful twist, a testament to her multifaceted spirit. This balance of softness and complexity, peppered with unexpected humor, makes her work a journey of constant evolution, rich in both emotion and insight.

Sonesta's writings are not just words on a page; they are a dance of contrasts and a celebration of life's diverse tapestry. Through her poetry, she invites readers to explore the profound and the playful, the serene and the stirring, always leaving them with a sense of peace, comfort, and introspection.

Beyond her poetic endeavors, Sonesta is a mentor and life coach, dedicated to empowering individuals to live authentically and embrace their full potential. Through her work with the Empowered Life Project (ELP), she strives to help people design lives filled with purpose, self-love, and growth. Her mission is to foster a sense of home within oneself, creating a foundation of strength and resilience.

Connect with Sonesta:

- **Sonesta's IG:** @sonestawildepoetry

- **ELP IG:** @empoweredlifeproject

- **Website:** sonestawilde.com

Chamomile and Lavender: Sips of Peace, Comfort, and Introspection
by Sonesta Wilde

Publisher: Sonesta Wilde
Kennesaw, Georgia
sonestawilde@gmail.com

ISBN: 979-8-9897696-3-6

Library of Congress Cataloging-in-Publication Data
Wilde, Sonesta.
Chamomile and Lavender: Sips of Peace, Comfort, and Introspection /
Sonesta Wilde. — 1st ed.
ISBN 979-8-9897696-3-6

Cover Design and Illustrations: Samantha Estimada

Printed in the United States of America

This book is a work of creative non-fiction. While it includes elements based on real experiences and observations, certain names, characters, and events have been changed or embellished for artistic purposes.

Content Warning: This book contains sensitive or potentially triggering themes such as grief, trauma, depression, suicide, and abuse. Reader discretion is advised. For mental health support, please refer to the resources listed on page 416 or contact local services available to you..

Disclaimer:
This book is intended for reflection and inspiration but is not a substitute for professional mental health support. If you are struggling, please seek help from a qualified professional.

www.ingramcontent.com/pod-product-compliance
Lightning Source LLC
Chambersburg PA
CBHW030350130626
46549CB00004B/1435